PORTUGUESE KNITTING

A historical & practical guide to traditional Portuguese techniques,
with 20 inspirational projects

ROSA POMAR

First published in Great Britain 2020 by
Search Press Limited
Wellwood, North Farm Road
Tunbridge Wells, Kent TN2 3DR

Originally published as *Malhas Portuguesas: História e prática do* tricot *em Portugal*
by Rosa Pomar
© 2013 Civilização Editora
English Translation by Burravoe Translation Services

Illustrations: Rita Cordeiro

ISBN 978-1-78221-721-3

If you have difficulty in obtaining any of the materials and
equipment mentioned in this book, then please visit the Search
Press website for details of suppliers: www.searchpress.com

*Dedicated to Irene, who taught me to knit and purl over thirty years ago,
and to the women everywhere who have shared their knowledge with me.*

Contents

Preface

It was only in 2009 that I first heard of Rosa Pomar.

That year, the public unrest that had stemmed from the protests against the closure of the Museu de Arte Popular (MAP – the Folk Art Museum), brought my attention to something I had been aware of but had not come across personally before: people completely different from the group who, like myself, either formally or informally, shared an interest in traditional Portuguese Crafts.

The texts by this group of people – from a wide range of career backgrounds – were testament to their fascination with the heritage of Portuguese Arts and Crafts, and they were protesting against the MAP's lack of connection with this multifaceted reality. Among these names was that of Rosa Pomar.

However, it was only through the exhibition 'Fios. Formas e Memórias dos Tecidos, Rendas e Bordados' [Threads, Forms and Memories of Fabrics, Lace and Embroidery], which I helped to curate, at the Instituto de Emprego e Formação Professional [Institute of Employment and Professional Training] at the FIL pavilion, that I had the chance to meet Rosa Pomar in person. Her criticisms, questions and comments showed me her expertise, passion and knowledge of the field of Portuguese handmade textiles.

With this encounter, I discovered Rosa Pomar's deep love for the history of Portuguese knitting; that the knowledge she has of indigenous breeds of sheep is greater than that of most vets; and that she criss-crosses the country wherever there is any kind of artisanal wool processing and production, wherever there is any kind of knitting – hats, babies' booties, gloves or sweaters.

Rosa Pomar wants to know and investigate everything connected with knitting and knitwear. She's as familiar with the cold of Montemuro and Estrela as she is with the many women from the Mirandês Plateau who spend their days working with wool, and who now consider her as a friend.

After several years of extensive research, her passion and love for an overlooked and undervalued area of Portuguese crafts has now resulted in a book – in this book, which for the first time ever explores and shares the huge variety of Portuguese knitted fabrics, and outlines their history, production methods and unique qualities.

Rosa Pomar's pioneering work has finally filled the gap in the very limited bibliography on textiles to date. The advertising slogan of over 30 years ago – *Minha lã, meu amor* [My wool, my love] – could have been created by Rosa Pomar. It would have been just perfect.

Ana Pires

Introduction

It is hard to define precisely when the idea for this book began to take shape. Thirty years ago – when I was just seven years old, an older cousin taught me the basics of knit and purl.

Around 2010 I took the decision to spend one day a week studying and writing about the subject, and this led to yet further questions. The first and most immediately obvious question related to the illustrations in the knitting books I had been using to try to learn from: why did the illustrations show a way of holding the yarn and needles so different from the way I did it? Then I wondered why some people knitted using the 'around the neck' [ao pescoço] method and others the 'English' [ao dedo] method. At the turn of this century, the internet opened up a huge window of knowledge about knitting in the USA, and this was soon followed by knitting styles from many other countries. This period reignited a worldwide interest in artisanal production that has continued to gain momentum and bear fruit. People who were already experienced knitters, as well as novices, were able – with just a click – to access a wealth of previously unfamiliar or inaccessible yarns and materials as well as related sites and publications. I treasured the *Complete Guide to Needlework* that I had inherited from my grandmother, and started collecting newly published knitting books from different countries – books with patterns that I actually felt like wearing, something totally different from the magazines available from Portuguese newsstands. This was followed by the publication of numerous other books on local techniques and patterns from other parts of the world including the Andes, Turkey and Scandinavia.

I have been interested in traditional Portuguese textiles for a long time. While my academic background (in history, with a brief stint in fine art) has fuelled my interest in production contexts and processes, my childhood – which was filled with tales of weaving and embroidery, knitting and crochet – also played an equally important role in my burgeoning interest in the field. The commentaries and images on my blog (aervilhacorderosa.com) over the past ten years illustrate this journey.

As I researched the historical and ethnographical bibliography on Portuguese textiles, it became clear that knitted fabrics had rarely been given the attention they deserved and had received in other countries. The few studies I did manage to find were those written by Leite de Vasconcelos and Vergílio Correia in the early 20th century, and the detailed notes on the traditional hats with earflaps from the Island of Madeira written by Luisa Gonçalves and Duarte Gomes in 2011; yet these cover only a tiny part of past and present knitting traditions. In terms of practical manuals published after the 1950s, the only one is Maria José Roxo's little-known but fascinating *Rendas "por música"* [*Lacework by Music*], published in 1985 by Civilização.

The aim of this book is not to have the final say on such a relatively under-studied subject, but to bring the almost unknown world of traditional Portuguese knitting to a wider audience. Additionally, from my own perspective as a knitter, it seeks to offer approaches and techniques that are more practical than academic. One of the project's original aims was precisely to create a first knitting manual using methods that will be familiar to the majority of Portuguese knitters, with the yarn around the neck or over the shoulder.

The first chapter of this book, *The History of Knitting*, references a range of printed sources from different fields and subjects and collates the information contained within to trace a chronology of the evolution of knitted textiles in Portugal. This highlights the fact that there is still relatively little research in the field to enable any wider perspective. However, there have been some intriguing 'discoveries', such as the realization that the gloves of Estêvão Anes Brochardo (image 2, page 14), the existence of which I only found out from Dr Paula Monteiro from the Laboratório de Conservação e Restauro José de Figueiredo [the José de Figueiredo Conservation and Restoration Laboratory], are, according to my research, the oldest known knitted pieces in the country.

The second chapter, *Knitting in Portugal*, was a bigger challenge. While, on the one hand, I wanted to cover all the bibliography on Portuguese ethnography and textile history, on the other, I also felt I needed to meet people whose knitting knowledge had never been formally recorded before. This without a doubt became the most important part of the entire process: learning from the hands of people throughout the country who have kept such things alive – Vilão hats, São Miguel caps, Serra de Ossa socks, Grades socks and Concha socks. This project has only been made possible through the kindness and generosity of so many people, who – from the Mirandês plateau to the islands of the Azores and Madeira – shared with me both their knowledge and their time. Direct access to historical pieces was also essential, and I am deeply grateful to several students who shared with me the socks, needles and other precious heirlooms that had been handed down to them over the years, and to the generosity of several museums. Of particular note among the latter is the Museu Nacional de Etnologia [National Ethnology Museum], which allowed me to look more closely at a range of pieces. The image research was an exciting and fruitful part of the work that uncovered previously unreferenced depictions of knitted items, such as the 1841 engraving which clearly shows a representation of a São Miguel island cap (image 29, page 52), and the photograph of a Corvo islander wearing the traditional woollen beret at the turn of the 20th century (image 27, page 50).

The third chapter, *Techniques*, is a short guide on how to knit in the Portuguese style, and offers practical suggestions for choosing yarns and tools. I have tried to prioritize giving clear illustrations of the techniques mentioned in the projects, and my friend Rita Cordeiro has helped to make this possible. Rita's illustrations have contributed to making this book an essential reference on Portuguese knitting. The techniques shown have been selected from a huge repertoire – one impossible to fully encompass in the scope of this particular project, so we have chosen to illustrate all of those required to make the patterns given in the chapter that follows. More experienced knitters will find their own ways of doing these using their own preferred techniques, but novices should also find what they need in order to progress. Despite this, even those with more knitting experience may be surprised by the way of working knit stitch that I learned in Mezio from D. Carolina da Costa.

The book concludes with the fourth chapter, *Patterns*, all of which – directly or indirectly – have been inspired by traditional Portuguese patterns, in their motifs, colours and materials. Above all, they have been made according to the most easy and intuitive way of knitting for all those who do it Portuguese style: mostly purling and in the round whenever possible. Some, like the Villain's Cap (page 99) or the Concha Socks (page 134), are shown in exactly the same way as I was taught with no changes. In both their form and function, they seem to me as fresh and relevant as when they were first made decades, or perhaps even centuries, ago.

A HISTORY OF KNITTING

A History of Knitting

Although the 20th century has seen an increasing number of reference books on handmade textiles, knitting has continued to be overlooked, and has remained a branch of Portuguese textile production that is still little known, despite the wealth of production, opportunity and interest.

Few books have been published about Portuguese weaving, lace or embroidery traditions and even fewer about Portuguese knitting. Portuguese ethnographers rarely paid any attention at all to knitting even though it was being done using the same materials, in the same places and by the same hands as other textiles they considered more worthy of their research.

There is, of course, a variety of reasons for this lack of engagement: on the one hand, knitting projects are in general smaller pieces – which by their very nature tend to be less eye-catching or desirable than items such as quilts or embroidered pieces. Their smaller dimensions match their lower visibility, as in the case of socks or purses. Another contributory factor to their low profile is that their manufacture does not require large tools such as looms, and neither is their creation limited to any specific location or season.

With a handful of exceptions, traditional knitted pieces didn't gain new uses or purposes that would have allowed them to be sold outside their traditional settings, as it happened in recent years with some embroidered and woven pieces. However, perhaps the underlying reason for this is that until only about two generations ago, knitting techniques – which are relatively easy to learn – were shared by all sectors of Portuguese society, and were familiar to most women. This meant that ethnographers (and everyone else) did not consider knitting as a skill that was in need of documenting and preservation. The Portuguese word *malhas* encompasses both knitting and crochet, two techniques that are related to each other and comprise one of the branches of the textile family.

Within the field of knitting, the oldest known technique is commonly known as *nalbinding* (where the fabric is produced with a needle similar to a sewing needle using short lengths of yarn), which, in Europe, dates back at least to the Roman occupation, and is still practised in certain areas of Scandinavia and the Middle East. Pieces produced using this technique look very similar to ordinary knitted fabric, and it can sometimes be difficult to differentiate between them. However, as far as we know, because no records of it have been found, *nalbinding* was not a technique used in Portugal. This book will only look at techniques and pieces that can be produced with two or more needles (knitting), and not at the one-needle techniques that are more commonly designated in Portuguese as crochet or 'hook lace'.

It seems that knitting has existed in one form or other for almost a thousand years. The oldest known knitted pieces are fragments that were probably made in Coptic Egypt before the 12th century, and a pair of socks from Egypt (now in the Textile Museum, Washington) that have been dated to the same century. Despite their age, these have the same design as those found in the West today. They were knitted from the toe up and feature two-colour stranded knitting. The construction and decorative features of these socks and the pieces previously referred to suggest that the technique was not a recent discovery, and that it had taken time to evolve and develop. These archaeological finds, many of which are small and difficult to date, make it impossible to date the invention of knitting any earlier than 1000 AD.

Researchers are generally in agreement that knitting was first invented in North Africa around the 11th century, and that it entered Europe via the Iberian Peninsula through Muslim intermediaries. The oldest dated European knitted pieces were found in Spain: a pair of pillows from the tombs of two of Alfonso X's children (image 1), and a pair of gloves belonging to Rodrigo Ximénez de Rada, the Archbishop of Toledo, who died in 1247. Studies suggest that both the pillows and the gloves were made by artisans from Al-Andaluz (part of the Iberian Peninsula that was under Muslim occupation).This belief is reinforced by the Arabic inscriptions on two of them, and by their exceptional quality in comparison with Christian textile production of the times. It is hard to know if knitting was still confined to specialist workshops by the middle of the 13th century, or whether it had already spread through the wider community; however, what is known is that garments worn by the kings and nobility of León at the time tended to be made from fabric of Muslim origin.[1] Nevertheless, it is not unreasonable to imagine that the general populace was already making their own knitted garments, even though they may have been more crudely produced and have used more accessible raw materials such as wool and flax.

The oldest knitted pieces found in Portugal to date, which are among some of the oldest in the world, are two pairs of gloves from the 14th century that belonged to Bishop Estêvão Anes Brochardo (Chancellor of D. Dinis and the Bishop of Coimbra, who died in 1318) (image 2), and to D. Gonçalo Pereira (the Archbishop of Braga, who died in 1348) (image 3). D. Estêvão's gloves were removed from his tomb in the old cathedral in Coimbra in the late 19th century and were restored by the Instituto dos Museus [the Institute of Museums] in the late 1960s.They are of exquisite quality, knitted in the round in fine silk yarn and decorated on the backs of both hands with multicoloured embroidery. The *Agnus Dei* [lamb of God], surrounded by flora and

fauna (little birds, rabbits and dogs), is depicted at the base of the embroidered image. The gloves are unique not only because of their age, but also for their beautiful embroidery.

The second pair of gloves, which belonged to D. Gonçalo Pereira, was removed in the 1990s from his tomb in Braga Cathedral, and was restored by the Abegg Foundation. They are currently on display at the Tesouro-Museu da Sé de Braga [Treasure Museum of Braga Cathedral]. They were also worked in the round using silk yarn, and have richly embroidered coloured wrist decorations. Both pairs are made of white or very light coloured yarn, as this was the standard for gloves worn by bishops until the 16th century, after which red or green became more common. The backs of D. Gonçalo Pereira's gloves would also have had medallions of metal or precious stones affixed to them (shown on the statue adjacent to the tomb), but these are likely to have been removed together with the other jewels that accompanied the body at an unknown time in the past.

Although these examples prove the existence of knitted pieces in Portugal in the 14th century, there is no evidence to suggest that either pair of gloves was produced in Portugal. Not only the nobility chose to dress mostly in imported fabrics, but also, as in the case of D. Gonçalo's gloves, the type of embroidery that decorated the wrists (*Opus Anglicanum*) points to a possibly British origin.[2]

A number of knitted fragments were recovered from an archaeological dig in the ossuary of the São Vicente de Fora Monastery in Lisbon, and the location in which they were found made it possible to fairly confidently date them as coming from the end of the Middle Ages and the Early Modern period.[3] Due to their age and the variety of stitches used, these finds are significant in the history of knitting in Portugal.

The oldest fragment (dated from around the 12th

1. Pillow from the tomb of D. Fernando de Lacerda, son of Alfonso X the Wise. Monastery of Las Huegas, Burgos, late 13th century.
2. Gloves belonging to Estêvão Anes Brochardo, Chancellor of D. Dinis and Bishop of Coimbra, early 14th century.
3. Pontifical gloves belonging to the Archbishop of Braga, D. Gonçalo Pereira, first half of the 14th century.

century) was made from linen yarn, probably back and forth on two needles, and features a zigzag diamond pattern formed by yarn overs and simple decreases (image 4). It is described as being part of a sock or stocking, although this interpretation requires further evidence to back it up. The other fragments date from the 16th century and show a variety of decorative motifs using cables, travelling stitches and purl stitches (image 5). All of these stitches remained in use over the following centuries and are still used today; however, they are rare proof of their use in such distant times. The lack of detailed research and knowledge of other pieces from the time makes it hard to understand clearly how knitting techniques spread throughout Portugal so widely; but they are likely to have followed a similar pattern as that seen over the rest of the Iberian Peninsula. The smaller garments made using the most common raw materials, flax and wool, were probably those that were disseminated first, both in Portugal and in the rest of Europe: caps, pockets, purses and gloves, and then socks; and these would have been produced depending on the availability of raw materials and the level of technical expertise, and would have been passed among the lower classes slowly over the following centuries. The nobility and the clergy had more sophisticated pieces, many of which were imported or commissioned from skilled craftspeople and were made from luxury threads – the Las Huelgas pillows and D. Gonçalo Pereira's gloves being early examples.

A group of paintings from the second half of the 14th century, which depict the Virgin Mary knitting, show that the technique was already in use. Most of the paintings are Italian and show circular knitting techniques using four or five needles and, in some cases, complex jacquard designs (image 6).

On the Iberian Peninsula, the oldest known representation of knitting is in a Spanish altarpiece made by Nicolás and Martín Zahortiga for the Colegiada de Borja [the Collegiate Church of Santa Maria in Borja] in Zaragoza between 1460 and 1477, which shows the Virgin Mary accompanied by a group of holy women. All those in the foreground are busy with different textile crafts, and one (on the right) is making a circular knitted piece using five needles, which could be a sock, with a white background and two bands decorated in red and black (image 7). The image, which is extremely detailed, places knitting in the context of a feminine domestic or monastic environment rather than that of a craftsman's workshop, where elaborate pieces were made for family or religious purposes.

In Catalonia in 1394 – approximately half a century earlier – a contract had been agreed that committed women to teaching their younger peers to make *calces d'agulla* [knitted stockings] over a four-year period.[4] This long apprenticeship suggests that the pieces were highly complex to make, particularly when – as we will see later – one considers that the making of simple socks and stockings over the centuries was undertaken even by young children, who learnt through imitation.

In the 15th and 16th centuries, and perhaps even earlier, there is evidence that knitted pieces became increasingly popular among the general populace. The most comprehensive works on the subject – *A History of Hand Knitting*, by Richard Rutt, and Irena Turnau's *History of Knitting Before Mass Production*, show the development of professional groups dedicated to creating knitwear in several European countries from the Late Middle Ages onwards, and there are numerous archaeological finds that show how knitting spread through much of Europe.

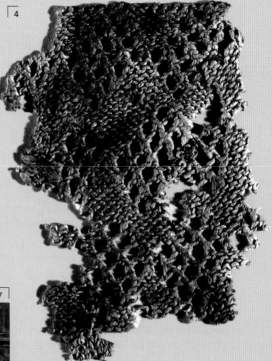

The most widespread garments were different kinds of caps, but pieces like knitted stockings, garters, sleeves, gloves and tunics are also mentioned in documents from the period, and survive in the collections of various museums. There are two important texts from the mid-16th century that lead one to believe a similar thing took place in Portugal: the *Sumário*, published in 1551,[5] and the *Grandeza e Abastança de Lisboa* of 1552,[6] listed the occupations of Lisbon's residents and numbers of each of them. The *Sumário* reports that in the category of manual occupations there were 173 trouser-makers, 15 hat-makers and 14 hood-makers. The *Grandeza e Abastança de Lisboa* mentions 80 trouser-sellers and 15 cap-sellers who made and sold caps, *gualteiras* (another kind of headwear) and children's cuffs. Although none of these terms state that the pieces were actually knitted, it is likely that they were in some cases. This idea is supported by the oldest names for these garments: *barretes*, *carapuças* and *gualteiras* – terms for different headgear used in texts by Gil Vicente – which are all described as being made from both cloth and leather, as well as in stocking stitch.[7] The same is seen on the other side of the border where, in 1611, the *Tesoro de la Lengua Castellana o Española* [the Treasury of the Spanish and Castilian Language] suggested that cuffs and caps were also often knitted[8] as were the *manguitas de meninos* and *mangas pequenas* [boys' cuffs and sleeves].[9,10] However, the trousers made by the trouser-makers, close-fitting garments that covered the leg from the foot to the top, and which led to the stockings of later centuries,[11] are assumed to have been made from woven rather than knitted fabric. The *Tesoro* refers more than once to *calças de aguja* [knitted trousers], particularly in the definition of the knitting needles themselves.[12] It should be remembered that the above-mentioned Catalan contract also confirms the production of knitted trousers from the end of the 14th century.

On the subject of the different kinds of caps, hoods, and other headgear, which were considered essential items of men's clothing at the time, there is a Portuguese illuminated manuscript from the early 16th century which shows one of the types of cap from that period, and which is clearly knitted (image 8). Very similar knitted hats with ear flaps are preserved in the Museu Marítimo de Ílhavo [Ílhavo Maritime Museum], which were worn by fishermen from the region until recently.

It is worth noting that in the 16th and 17th centuries the word *malha* appears to have been used only for military clothing (the mail made from chains – chainmail), and to refer to fishing (and other kinds of) nets. It is only at the end of the 18th century that we find the term used with its current meaning: the kind of stitch that is used to make socks and other garments.[13] The oldest texts, both in Portugal and throughout the rest of the Iberian Peninsula, make a distinction between knitted pieces and woven fabrics, with the former using the expression *de agulha* [by needle], and later, *de meia* or *de ponto de meia* [of/by stocking stitch]; and the latter as *de pano* [of cloth]. This development led to transformations in dress, and showed the increasing influence of knitting in the 17th century. This terminology is still used today in rural contexts – *fazer meia* [lit. making sock] is still the preferred term to describe the act of knitting, and *renda de agulha* [lit. needle lace] is the common way of referring to knitted lace (referred to on page 62). *Tricotar* [knit] and *tricot* [knitting] – terms derived from the French – were introduced by the educated classes, and only came into common usage in the cities from the mid-20th century.

8

9

quoniam dns iesus ❦   erbū caro panem

8. Illumination from the Breviário da Condessa de Bertiandos [the Breviary of the Countess of Bertiandos], (detail) 16th century.
9. Man with knitted cap. Playing card, 18th century.

It was also in the 16th century that knitting spread to other continents carried there by the Portuguese and Spanish. Knitting was unknown in the Americas before Columbus and was only taken up by the indigenous populations in many regions after colonisation. They combined the new technique with their advanced knowledge of spinning, weaving and dyeing to produce, to this day, highly elaborate pieces that also often include motifs from their Hispanic heritage. The best known among these are the traditional Andean chullos (hats), knitted in the Portuguese style with the yarn passed behind the neck. In Japan, knitting (or at least the first knitted fabrics) also seems to have been introduced by Portuguese navigators and traders: not only are there no records or archaeological finds prior to the arrival of the Portuguese (in the 16th century), but also the word *meriasu* or *meyasu* (メリヤス), which signifies both the knitted stitch and the fabric, comes from the Portuguese *meia* [sock].[14]

In England in 1589, William Lee invented the first mechanical knitting machine. Similar in size and appearance to a conventional loom, the first versions made it possible to knit a fabric five times faster than was possible manually. Lee's machine, which was considered one of the most important innovations prior to the Industrial Revolution, began to be used throughout much of Europe within the following century, and in the last quarter of the 17th century there were already knitting looms in operation all over the Iberian Peninsula. The speed at which these machines were able to work made them very attractive, despite the fact that they were much more limited in terms of stitch variety and shaping the fabric than manually produced pieces.

Until the end of the 18th century, mechanically produced fabrics were made in strips that then had to be cut and sewn into the desired shape, but those produced manually could both create and shape the pieces simultaneously. All other tasks involved in knitted products of the times – the spinning and the finishing required (such as the felting and carding of finished pieces) were entirely manual.

In Portugal, knitting looms were introduced in the mid-17th century, and there were several knitting looms used in workshops linked to the Sedas do Rato factory in Lisbon in 1678, which employed at least 300 workers.[15] Numerous hosiery factories in Lisbon, particularly Sobral de Monte Agraço, Oeiras and Tomar were referenced over the following century.[16] Manufacturers, weavers, craftsmen and apprentices in the hosiery industry are mentioned in various processes at the time of the 18th century Inquisition, and are almost always associated with the country's main textile production centres, both for wool (in Estremoz) and silk (Bragança, Freixo de Espada and Cinta). This idea of a factory needs to be put into context here, as it used to mean something rather different. All of the looms used for these hosiery factories were set up in the houses or workshops of the craftspeople who operated them, and who were assisted by their apprentices or family – they were not in large-scale industrial units. These workshops produced a similar variety of pieces to those of earlier times: socks, gloves, caps, as well as *manguitas* [cuffs] and *calções* [hose].[18]

From the 17th century, manually produced textiles were made alongside those produced mechanically. The latter became increasingly popular as production techniques were perfected and disseminated, and made products more affordable. The continuing organization and mechanization of the textile industry over the 18th and 19th centuries led to new distribution channels and to the use of new raw materials: the wool, linen and silk that had been used previously was joined by cotton from the colonies, which was easier to work with and was ideal for the new machines.

The above-mentioned proto-industrial textiles developed in Portugal while at the same time the country was importing large quantities of knitted wool and silk garments from different parts of Europe (Germany, France and Spain). Strictly manual knitting kept its place and coexisted with imports and manufactured items. In a letter addressed to the governor of the province, Diniz de Melo e Castro, in 1678, Dom Pedro II offers an interesting view on knitted products by the women of Alentejo, recommending that women focus on spinning wool, breeding silkworms *and knitting socks as these occupations were useful for the development of manufacturing*.[19] At the turn of the following century, customs records for the city of Lisbon mention the importation of, among many other products, hose from Lamego (in the district of Viseu) and Pinhel (the district of Guarda), which were probably produced manually. Mondim da Beira, situated 15 kilometres south of Lamego, was renowned in the early 19th century for its manual production of a range of woollen garments, and became known as *Mondim das Meias*.[20] The importance of these centres, as well as the variety of garments in circulation in Portugal at the beginning of the 18th century, is clear from Bluteau's entry to the first major Portuguese language dictionary:[21] *a thousand styles of knitted socks come to us from all over Europe in different styles, fashion and material; socks made of wool, silk, linen and cotton, and in addition to woollen socks from Lamego and the monks' socks from Pinhel, every day sees new strangely named stockings from England, the Netherlands, Hamburg, and Paris: fine and semi-fine fabrics, children's socks, etc*. In other parts of the *Vocabulário*, Bluteau also mentions the *meyas de cabrestilho* [a kind of legging], a name by which they were known until the 20th century (*these are worn under other legwear and have only a strap, but no foot nor heel*), and the unusual *meyas de pantorrilha* [calf socks], which by that time had already fallen into disuse.[22]

In the Portugal of the 18th and 19th centuries, there were both mechanically and manually produced knitted garments available of varying quality: the former were often more luxurious products imported for the wealthier classes who were their principal consumers, and the latter were typically locally produced for the general populace.

The survival and importance of hand knitting relates to the specifics of Portuguese textile manufacturing as a whole: the majority of the population consumed textiles produced by small workshops or at home, made from locally sourced wool and linen and sold through small local markets. This framework of weak industrial development and geographical isolation explains in part the continued use until today of such a wide range of knitting practices, techniques and traditions.

Throughout the 19th century, knitting as a taught skill is frequently referred to in texts on the education of girls from all walks of life. We know that *fazer meia* [lit. making socks] (an expression which, in Portuguese, is almost always used as a synonym of knitting), sewing and embroidery were considered essential skills for young women. Among those from more privileged backgrounds, working *with the needle* showed an approach to life that was suitably secluded and home-focused. However, girls from more humble backgrounds could use their skills not only to make garments for their families, but also to trade and as a means of earning a living when necessary; it was also something that the elderly, orphans and the disabled could do.

The following are two examples of many: In his *Cartas dirigidas a uma senhora ilustre encarregada da instituição de uma jovem princesa* {*Letters addressed to a distinguished lady in bringing up a young princess*] (1867), Almeida Garrett wrote: *I therefore believe that from the age of six, sitting at their mothers' feet, little girls should start practising with their needles for one hour, twice a day; this in order that they become used to the constant and most precious occupation of their sex (...). It is also essential to teach them to knit from a very young age: (...) it is impossible to knit fast and well if one has not played with the needles since the age of seven. This is because one has to consider the children's futures; what happens when a beautiful little girl of ten becomes a grandmother of sixty? Although her eyes may be weaker and can no longer count the cambric or fine threads, she will still be able to make so many beautiful and useful things and do so swiftly and perfectly without even looking.*[23] Knitting was just as important for the state-provided education for vulnerable orphans – both girls and boys: *(...) the girls need their carers to teach them sewing, knitting, and other skills appropriate for their sex and age, and as their education is excellent they find themselves much sought after (...).Boys also learn how to knit, and sometimes how to card flax, hemp and wool, and to work in different trades (...) and the girls learn to knit, sew, spin, weave, make ribbon and lace, and every other kind of needle-work.*[24]

Ethnographic texts show how knitting was a constant occupation for Portuguese women in rural Portugal, not only as an isolated activity but as something done while performing other tasks – for example, while keeping watch over the cattle, carrying heavy loads on their heads or children on their backs: *They knit at home, in the street, when going to the well or while travelling from one village to another, while running errands, and do not waste a single moment, because here* [in Mondim das Meias] *it is not just about creating something*

necessary, but about an industry that provides people's bread and butter.[25]

For a long time, right up to the start of the 20th century, knitting was seen primarily as something to occupy the hands whenever they were not occupied with any other task. Although as a full-time occupation it was not very lucrative, it was possible to profitably use non-productive times, breaks and the evenings to supplement the family budget.

Scholarly interest in regional customs and clothing from the late 18th century onwards has bequeathed numerous images of men and women wearing knitted garments. One of the oldest of these is in the collection of the Museu Nacional de Arte Antiga [National Museum of Ancient Art] and is a deck of playing cards that shows a range of traditional figures, many of which (with an emphasis on the seafaring professions) show figures wearing knitted hats (image 9).

Publications dedicated to knitting appeared in Portugal in the 20th century. In 1932, the women's magazine *Modas e Bordados* [*Fashion and Embroidery*] promised its readers *patterns of varying levels of difficulty, not only for experts (...) but also for those with less ability.* The patterns published in subsequent issues are often no more than images of certain stitches with suggestions on how to use them. Even in a context of literate urban women – who would have been the magazine's target audience, knitting was still something best learned through imitation, from samples and made pieces that could be kept for future reference (image 10).

The first knitting book by a Portuguese author with original content was the *Método de Fazer Malhas* [*Method of Knitting*] by Fernando Baptista de Oliveira, published in 1952 and reprinted at least twice over the following years. *O Tricot sem Mestre* [*Knitting without a Teacher*] by Lília da Fonseca, was published in 1957. Similarly to contemporary

10. "The most fashionable knitwear", *Lavores e Arte Aplicada* magazine, 1945.

publications in other countries, both reflected an era when off-the-peg clothing had not yet fully replaced homemade garments, and when knitting was still more than just a hobby and was a technique known and practised by women from all backgrounds. (images 11 and 12).

The following decades saw a proliferation of translations of foreign knitting magazines. The 1980s, which was marked by a boom in artificial materials as well as by a renewed interest in homemade fabrics, saw the launch of the only Portuguese magazine with original content – *Arrancar, Moda em Tricot* [*Get Going, Fashion in Knitting*], which was published for five years by the yarn companies Arrancada and Fisipe. Its inaugural edition in 1985 began thus: *This is the first time our country has produced a wholly national knitting and fashion magazine. Portuguese women are, without a shadow of a doubt, some of the most talented artisans in the world. The small yet exquisite pieces created (often without fanfare), by such able hands deserve greater encouragement, respect and renown.*

11. *Método de Fazer Malhas [Method of Knitting], by* Fernando Batista de Oliveira, 1952.
12. *O Tricot sem Mestre [Knitting without a Teacher] by* Lília da Fonseca, 1957.

1. Feliciano, 2005.
2. We would like to thank Dr Paula Monteiro from the Instituto dos Museus e da Conservação (Institute of Museums and Conservation) for her invaluable help with information about these pieces and particularly about the discovery of Estêvão Anes Brochardo's gloves.
3. Cunha, 1998; Fernando Ferreira, 1983.
4. Stanley, 1997, p. 59.
5. Oliveira, 1987.
6. Buarcos, 1990.
7. Silva, 1789.
8. *Bonetero, el que haze bonetes, y unos son de lana y aguja, de que se haze en Toledo, y en otras partes, gran cargazon para fuera de España: y otros de pano (...). Gorra: La forma de la gorra es redonda, y en tiempos atras se traya llana sobre la cabeça, y era, o de aguja, o de paño (...).* [Bonetero, the person who makes bonnets, and some are made with wool and needle, in Toledo and in other parts, great cargo for outside of Spain: and others of cloth (...). Cap: The shape of the cap is round, and in times gone by it was plain on the head, and was either needle or cloth.] Covarrubias, 1611.
9. Bluteau, 1728.
10. Cuff: Knitted piece to protect shirt arms and wrists from soiling. Silva, 1789.
11. The word *meia* is derived from *meia calça*, used to designate short trousers that stop at the knee.
12. *Llamanse tambien agujas unos hierrecicos delgados con que se hazen calças de punto, que llaman de aguja.* [They are also called thin, steel needles, with which knitted (or needle) stockings are made...] Covarrubias, 1611.
13. Silva, 1789.
14. Kim, 1976.
15. Bastos, 1960, p. 220.
16. Macedo, 1982, p. 153.
17. Case numbers 2263 and 3450 from the Coimbra Inquisition, 7206, 10784, 9994 and 11602 from the Lisbon Inquisition, among others.
18. Neves, 1827, p. 287.
19. Dias, 1953, p. 26.
20. Correia, 1916.
21. Bluteau, 1728.
22. They were used in the past, and made in such a way that the part that covered the calf of the leg was padded, or used thicker yarn, so as to enlarge the calf or pad it, which is why they were called *Meyas de panturrilha* [calf hose].Bluteau, 1728.
23. Garrett, 1867.
24. Pinto, 1828, pp. 110 and 121.
25. Correia, 1916.

LAVOR
tricot
PORTUGAL

KNITTING IN
PORTUGAL

Introduction

The most well-known Portuguese knitting technique still in use today is commonly known as *tricot ao pescoço* [round-the-neck knitting] or *ao ombro* [shoulder]. This means that the yarn from the ball is passed around one finger and then either behind the neck, or through a hook or pin attached to the chest, and the thread is then moved onto the needles through repeated left-thumb movements (see chapter 3). As it is passed around the neck or through a pin and secured to the finger, the yarn keeps its tension and is ready for use (image 1).

In Europe, this form of knitting is traditional only in the most southern regions. There are records of knitters from Portugal to Armenia who use the neck or pin method. This is also the case in areas of Spain, Italy, Montenegro, Albania, Macedonia, Greece, Romania, Bulgaria, Turkey, Armenia (and Algeria in Northern Africa), but it seems that it is only in Portugal that this technique is more popular than any other.

Having been introduced into the Americas by the Iberian colonizers, the round-the-neck method is still used occasionally across Latin America, from Brazil to the Andes (image 2). Of course, not everyone in Portugal did or does still knit the same way today.

In the northeast of the country, until the first half of the 20th century, the supported needle technique was still used. In this form of knitting, rather than the right-hand needle being held in the right hand, it is held in a fixed position on the right side of the body. A special device called a knitting sheath was used to keep the needle in position, and was relatively well known throughout Europe (Spain, France, Greece, the United Kingdom, etc.) in different shapes and materials, which we will look at later.

It is more common to find knitters who use the round-the-finger technique, or what is normally called the 'continental' technique (where the yarn is passed through the left hand), and the 'English technique' (where the yarn is passed through the right hand) in larger towns and cities, and this is likely either due to foreign influences or to family traditions, and as they appear to have been considered more refined ways of knitting.

The fundamental difference between Portuguese knitting and other techniques is that when using the round-the-neck (or pin) technique, purl stitch is much easier and faster to do than knit stitch. The opposite is true for all other techniques, where knit stitch is easier to make than purl stitch. This difference also affects the way circular pieces are knitted: knitters using the Portuguese method will in general choose to knit from behind, that is, always in purl.

The Portuguese method is considered by some experts to be a more recent technique than others, although this theory is not proven. The fact that this is the most common knitting technique in Latin America suggests that it has been used at least since colonial times.

However, the geographical dispersion of knitting throughout the regions around the Mediterranean and countries neighbouring those where the oldest knitted pieces have been found (Egypt), suggests that its origins are significantly older.

1.   Woman knitting a sock, Pitões das Júnias, 2011.
2.   Woman knitting fabric, Şirinci, Turkey, 2011.

Materials

Needles

We are five sisters,
All as good as the best,
But one of us is bare
And takes from the rest.[1]

Although the knitting needles sold in Portugal are now almost all imported and the same as those used in other countries (and despite the fact that YouTube has largely replaced mothers and grandmothers as a teacher, and has increasingly influenced the spread of Anglo-Saxon knitting techniques), one has only to leave urban conurbations to see how, together with Portuguese techniques, the tradition of working with hooked needles has continued. These needles have a normal knitting tip on one end and a crochet hook on the other end, and have different names depending on the region – *farpa*, *pega*, *gancho*, *mosca*, *garavata*, and so on. To make socks and other circular knitted pieces, a set of five identical needles (known as a *baralho*, or *jogo*) is used, with a hook at one end and the usual tip at the other. The stitches are worked with the hook, which pulls the yarn in an easier and speedier way than a regular knitting tip. In the left hand, the stitches slide easily off the normal knitting tip. With the continual rotation of the needle from the left hand to the right hand, the orientation of the needles continues naturally. When knitting back and forth, as is the case for the lace border shown on page 63, both hooks are held facing inwards. The use of point-hook needles makes it possible to create pieces swiftly, as the needle in the right hand only moves to the left and right, and is always held parallel to the left-hand needle, and this is impossible to do with standard knitting needles. The hooks also make it possible to create certain lace stitches that cannot

be created using standard needles, and this has led to a range of stitches that often differ from those found in other countries.

Traditional knitting needles tend to be homemade or made by local artisans. Throughout the country, one can find knitting needles made from such things as old umbrella ribs and even old bicycle spokes (image 3). Metal wire (iron, steel, copper) is the most commonly used material, but it is not the only one. Wood, which is also easy to access and simple to work with, was often used to make needles until up to only a few decades ago, and this is supported by the stories of several women from Mezio and Nisa, who told us that, as children, they had not been allowed to use metal needles, for fear of losing them. This meant that girls often learned to whittle their own needles from heather or any other available wood. Needles could also be made from bone or tortoiseshell (image 4).

Knitting pin

The knitting pin is a practical, industrial object, but a tool that has become an art form and taken on magical and religious connotations making it a kind of amulet – almost like a cross.[2] The knitting pin (also known as a *tecedor*) is an accessory used in Portuguese over-the-shoulder knitting. It is a small device affixed to the chest near the left shoulder through which the yarn is passed to maintain the tension of the yarn. It can be something as simple as a bent hairpin or safety pin, but it can also take more elaborate forms made from wood, bone, fruit stones, shells or clay (image 5). The use of decorated pins was a discussion point for ethnographers in the first half of the 20th century. Leite de Vasconcelos, Vergílio Correia and Luís Chaves referred to the use of a pin as an accessory associated with knitting on numerous occasions, and emphasized the artistic

3. Hand-made needles, Reguengos de Monsaraz (1980), Alvito (2011) & Gralhas (2011).
4. Whalebone needles, Azores, 20th century.
5. Bone knitting pins.

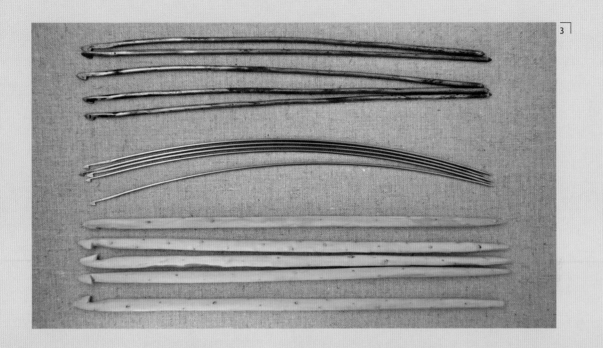

and symbolic interest in these pieces particularly in the region of Alentejo, where young men often made them as gifts for their girlfriends. It is in Alentejo that such carefully carved wooden pins – in the form of acorns, baskets and chairs (among other things), continue to be used until today, although of course they are less common. Until the early 20th century in Estremoz, painted clay and metal pins in the shape of popular characters (priests, soldiers, the Virgin Mary, etc.) continued to be made, and pieces can be found in the collection of the Museu de Arte Popular [Museum of Popular Art].

Knitting sheath

Along with the clogs, the knitting sheath is made and prepared by José Bernardino Alves, from the village of Babe in the centre of Lombada (Bragança); *he is the only person dedicated to making these for the old women who still knit using this process.* (1933)[3]

As previously mentioned, the knitting sheath is a tool that fell into relative disuse in Portugal over the first half of the 20th century, at a similar time to it falling out of favour in the rest of Europe. Ethnographic collections in several Portuguese museums include examples from Trás-os-Montes. We also know that these were reproduced as widely as the region of Tarouca, where Vergílio Correia registered them in 1916 under the term *chuço*.[4]

The sheath is a thin wooden cylinder, 20–30cm (8–11¾in) long, with a hole at one end to allow it to hold a narrow knitting needle firmly (image 6). In some cases, they are simply made from carved wood, but there are other examples with decorative touches that provide greater longevity. These are secured to the waist on the right of the body under the waistband of the skirt. This device is associated with the commonly called English style or right-hand knitting. Although it had been thought that people had stopped using knitting sheaths, the technique of supported knitting has actually continued to be used in villages in the region of Miranda do Douro until today, where the tip of the needle on the right is supported against the stomach and held in the same position throughout the project without any other aid. This way of working is very similar to the common Spanish tradition of working with the right-hand needle firmly tucked under the right arm and against the body. Some very elderly women from Trás-os-Montes still recall using the supported knitting technique, and say that it was most commonly used by shepherdesses who would knit as they were watching over their cattle.

Other accessories

While the above-mentioned items are those most directly related to knitting production, they are of course not the only ones. Of note are the *caninhas* (small canes) used in the region of Alentejo to protect the work in rest periods (image 7). They are a very simple accessory consisting of two hollow sections of cane or bone that are blocked at one end. Each one has a hole next to the opening, which holds a small thread or yarn. When not in use, the ends of the needles are stored inside the cases and the two threads are loosely knotted together, which prevents the knitted fabric from slipping off the needles and the needles from getting lost. The small canes are mentioned by Leite de Vasconcelos, who reports having seen them used in Alentejo and in Spain under the name of *preguiçosas* [lazy ones] or *agulheiros* [needle cases].[5]

Finishing techniques

The finish of knitted garments in the past was a key element of the process of making them. While nowadays we value and seek lightness and elasticity in knitwear, longevity and thermal qualities were the priorities of the past, and these rely in part on good finishing techniques. This explains why traditional woollen stockings, hats and sweaters tend to be so dense and have little elasticity. These results are achieved not only by using very fine needles, but also by slightly fulling/felting the knitted garments. Wooden sock blockers present in several museum collections are the remaining evidence of these practices. They consist of boards of pine or other wood about 1cm (½in) thick, cut to the shape and size the finished garment should have (image 8). The blockers we know of are from the region of Beira Alta, which in the past was known for its important production and trade in woolen socks. Once completed, the socks were washed and, while still damp, were placed over the blockers, and left to dry and take shape. They were then pressed between two planks, and were finally sewn to each other at both ends using contrasting coloured thread.[6]

The famous *Campino* [cow-herder] and fishermen's hats that are currently made in Castanheira de Pêra continue to be finished using this method in a process that gives them their characteristic final shape. The same method is found on the island of Corvo (see page 51), where the traditional berets are still shaped using water and a wire rim.

After drying, depending on the kind of wool used, the pieces can also be carded to lift and fluff the surface of the fabric in order to make them softer and more impermeable (see page 118).

Raw materials

The predominant raw materials presently used in traditional Portuguese knitting are wool and cotton.

Wool

Wool is the primary raw material for knitting. On the one hand, the process of creating yarn is relatively simple and swift (compared for example with that of flax), and can be undertaken quickly by a single person. Additionally, no other fibre offers the same versatility, which explains its continued use over the centuries.

Wool offers thermal insulation even when damp; it is elastic and malleable, but also resistant to continued usage without losing its shape. Wool is available in several different natural colours and it can also be easily dyed. It can also be spun to any desired thickness without needing anything other than a simple wooden spindle.

In some Portuguese regions, knitting is still done using wool that has been processed entirely by hand. Socks and caps are still made using homespun wool that comes from the family sheep that graze on the mountains nearby, and is washed in the river or an outdoor tank. These traditions can only be kept alive providing the pieces still hold some relevance, while the local folk traditions still include them in their outfits, and while sales through craft fairs and cooperatives encourage people to continue making them in their spare time – while watching the cattle – 'Just a few more stitches...'. So, in the north of the Serra da Estrela, in villages like Mezio (Castro Daire), Bucos (Cabeceiras de Basto) and Paredes do Rio (Montalegre), there are still women who carry on the wool processing techniques to make the yarn for their knitwear – from the raw material to a ball of yarn ready

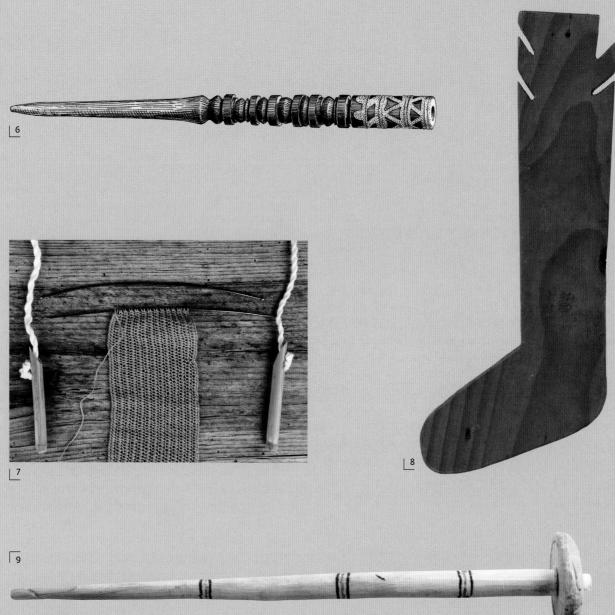

to knit. This process, albeit with significant regional variations, involves the following: after shearing, which is done in the spring (and, in the case of longhaired breeds, sometimes again in the autumn), the wool is selected and the dirtiest parts are discarded. The wool is then soaked in hot water, which cleans the fibres of most of the lanolin (the natural greases that protect and waterproof the wool). After this, it is carefully washed under cold running water. The wool is then squeezed out and left to dry, normally for several days. Once dry, it is then prepared for spinning. This process may simply be teasing (an operation known in different regions as *abrir*, *esguedelhar*, *escarpear*, *carbenar* or *carmear*, where the wool fibres are manually separated from each other), or it may be a more complex process where the wool fibres are separated by beating them, oiled and softened, and then carded or combed (using carders or combs) – to create homogeneous portions of wool (called *pastas*, *betas* or *panadas*) that are ready for spinning. Hand spinning survives mainly in its oldest and simplest traditional form – using a spindle and distaff, or even just a spindle (image 9). Although less common than spindles, spinning wheels, which spread throughout Europe from the 13th century onwards, were and still are used in Portuguese villages up and down the country. The last stage in the thread production is to ply two strands of yarn together. To do this, the two threads are skeined together and then twist is added using the spinning wheel or a spindle that in some cases is adapted for this purpose, or made specifically for this operation.

The wool yarn can be knitted in its different natural colours, or it can be dyed. The trade of dyer is as old as the Portuguese nation itself, even though the use of certain colours was restricted to only the wealthier members of society due to the high price of raw materials. As of the 19th century, with the discovery of aniline dyes, it became much easier to dye wool and other fibres in a wider variety of colours.

Traditional knitted garments are generally made using undyed yarn nowadays, but there are some exceptions. There are numerous references to both women and men in the north of Portugal wearing brightly coloured striped socks up until the mid-20th century. There are also still some villages that have kept up the practices of wool dying using plants and other accessible substances: chestnut shells, pomegranate husks, alder bark, some species of mushroom and lichen, rockroses (*Cytinus hipocistis*), dandelions (*Taraxacum officinale*), and sumac, and so on. The most common mordant used to fix the dye is copper sulphate, which in the villages is often known as *capa rosa*.

Cotton

Fine cotton yarn, commonly known as *linha*, is still widely used to make stockings and socks, lace and throws throughout the country. Its use became widespread from the 18th century onwards, as mechanically spun cotton was introduced to the country and gradually replaced the use of flax. Mercerized cotton yarn is used for knitting and crocheting nowadays, and it comes in different thicknesses depending on the kind of project for which it is needed. Brightly coloured cotton socks, either plain or patterned, were still worn throughout the region of Alentejo until just a few decades ago (image 10).

Flax

Along with wool, flax was the main raw material used to make traditional clothing in Portugal. The process of making yarn from flax is lengthy and demanding, and gradually fell into disuse as off-the-peg garments began to replace those that were homemade. Though flax spinning still survives, there are few examples of knitted garments made from it, and even fewer in national ethnographic collections. However, we do know that it was commonly used between the 16th and early 20th century when flax garments were still worn by the men and women from Minho – the main production region. The practice is evident in some of the popular knitting rhymes collected by Maria Emília de Vasconcelos,[7] such as the following, collected in 1938, by Viana do Castelo:

I really don't want the stockings of silk
That the master has promised to give me.
All that I want are the ones made of flax
Of the earth, and as humble as me.

Rags

As early as the 16th century, throughout the country, old clothes and other leftover fabrics were cut into strips and used for weaving. These strips were also used in some regions to make knitted rugs and throws, both as the main raw material, and in the form of shorter pieces that are intertwined within stitches.

The rags are sometimes twisted on a spindle before being knitted, which gives greater resistance and a more uniform appearance.

Pita

The fibres extracted from the leaves of the Aloe plant (*Agave americana*) were used to make lace, especially in the regions of the Azores and the Algarve. The Aloe plant is not indigenous to the area, and although it was primarily introduced as an ornamental species, it was also used to produce raw materials for textile production. Its fibres reach a maximum of 1 metre (1 yard), and have to be carefully joined to one another to create a useable yarn. In the 18th century, Bluteau referred to this fibre as being used as a raw material for sock production.[8] In the Azores, pita thread was the basis of a flourishing domestic industry in the 19th century, used to make shawls and other lace pieces that were generally made for export to the USA. There appear to be no examples of these in any museum collection in Portugal; however, it would be interesting to look into this subject more deeply.

The earliest reference to these pieces we have found is from 1867, where there is a passage from the book *A Trip to the Azores or Western Islands*, which describes the profusion of domestic textile production among the peasant women of the Azores: *They manufacture shawls, capes, veils, and other articles of ladies' apparel, from the fibres of the aloe, in black, white, and red*.[9]

In 1903, in an album dedicated to the Azores,[10] the production of lace made from pita is described thus: *One industry that has more or less continued, even if on a modest scale, since that date is pita lace, and until today it has consistently high sales in America. These delicate pieces, woven with the threads from Aloe leaves, are the product of huge dedication and effort, and they are not only admired for their incomparable quality but also for their soft, delicate lightness.* Ten years earlier, in 1893, the North American fashion magazine *Harper's Bazaar* dedicated an article

10. Women's cotton stockings made by Bela Celeste, Alcáçovas, Viana do Alentejo, 20th century.
11. Pita thread shawl, 19th century.

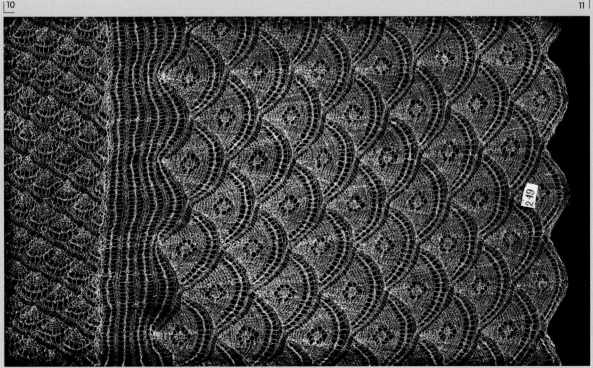

Types and traditions

to this kind of lace work and wrote that their patterns were created by local women[11] (image 11). In the region of Aljezur in the Algarve, they make (or have made until at least very recently) doilies made from pita. These pieces are referred to by Glória Marreiros in her fascinating book *Viveres, Saberes e Fazeres Tradicionais da Mulher Algarvia* [*Traditional Habits, Knowledge and Crafts of Women from the Algarve*],[12] which describes the process of extracting the fibres: *the women gathered the leaves and beat them with a mallet. They then extracted the juice from the plant. (...) The leaves were washed and put outside to cure in the sun and the open air for several weeks. The leaves were then washed again, separated into threads, and put out to dry on a sheet. After drying, each thread was separated one by one and joined with a "weaver's knot". The yarn was then blocked using a skein winder.*

Silk

Due to its cost, silk garments were nearly always restricted to the wealthiest, although Leite de Vasconcelos does mention it as one of the raw materials used in domestic sock production.[13] Silk thread continues to be hand-produced in Freixo de Espada à Cinta to this day, although it is not used for knitwear.

The production of traditional knits survives in various parts of the country, and there is a surprising variety. Some of the garments that are still produced today follow century-old patterns with few or no changes, and use techniques that have been passed on orally or through observation rather than via any written instruction or formal teaching. These techniques, seen, for example, in the Corvo island berets and the Serra de Ossa socks, which will be looked at in greater detail later on, are now only produced by a handful of elderly women, and run the risk of being forgotten before having been given the attention and study they so rightly deserve.

Over the following pages I will try to give a detailed description of several pieces produced nationally, grouped according to type. This kind of extensive research on the knitted artefacts of the villages of Portugal, and on the tools and techniques used to produce them, continues to be ongoing and urgent. The examples shown here have been chosen based on years of personal research, the ethnographic bibliography available, museum collections to which I have been granted access, and – most importantly – through direct contact with people from up and down the country who have so generously agreed to share their knowledge with me: people from institutions who granted me access to collections and information, and people in their own homes, or sitting outside in the sunshine, who – with yarn and needles in hand – carry on the traditional way of doing things.

This study cannot possibly be comprehensive, as information is scarce in some areas but abundant in others; however, this can only be expected in such a pioneering investigation into the previously neglected subject of Portuguese knitting. This book has prioritized pieces with notably regional characteristics, and has not touched on those whose production was mainly inspired by knitting manuals or magazines. It has also given preference to patterns for everyday and traditional knitwear over those that are merely decorative or made as a hobby.

Socks

Here we do not talk
About the lives of others
All we want
Is to make socks, socks!

Rose of the figs has a tongue made of rags
It is said that her man swallowed a frog!
Is it true?...
I don't know...

(refrain)

Yes, it is true, I heard
He swallowed a frog without even knowing!
Is it true?...
I don't know...

(refrain)

Rita made that cake
Gave the evil-eye to our Manel
Is it true?...
I don't know...

(refrain)

Tell Gertrude to not look back,
Only she knows how to deal with the boy
Is it true?...
I don't know...

(refrain)[14]

The term *fazer meia* (literally 'sock making') is synonymous in Portugal with knitting. *Ponto de meia* (stocking/stockinette stitch) is the main stitch used for the majority of pieces. Knitted socks give rise to the widest variety of techniques, patterns and stitches, and many different and unusual words survive to name them: *meias*, *miotes*, *miucos*; *peúgas*, *piúcos*, *pinças*; *carpins*, *canos*, *coturnos*, and so on. There are socks both with and without feet, ankle socks, over-the-knee socks, socks made from coarse or fine wool, single-colour and multicoloured patterned socks, simple socks and intricate socks of lace, socks that are worn under clothing and those that are designed to be worn outside trousers to protect against the cold, hard-wearing socks made for labouring in the fields and delicate stockings to be worn on special occasions – the variety is almost endless (image 12).

Virtually every one of these styles follows a common set of rules: in general they start at the top and finish at the toe (or in the case of footless socks, at the ankle), and are worked using five needles, always purling on the wrong side as this is the preferred method for Portuguese knitting in the round. The leg part is either cylindrical or conical and close fitting for longer socks; and the foot is made in six steps: the back of the heel [the *taloeira*, *talão* or *mão travessa*], the base of the heel (called *capuchinho* in the Montemuro mountains and *gorros* in the Mirandes plateau), the edges [*cantos*], *minguados* or *cunhas* under the ankles, the cylindrical or slightly conical instep and, finally, the toe-piece – called *mates* or *minguados*).

The cuff is almost always in a different stitch from the rest of the leg, either for aesthetic reasons, or to provide greater elasticity and make them easier to pull on and prevent them from slipping down.

Many socks have a vertical line that runs from top to bottom and that signals the start of each round. This line, commonly known as the *revesilho*, is achieved by alternating a knit stitch with a purl stitch for the first stitch of each round, or alternatively always in knit stitch.

12

13

14

12. Woman from Minho (northwest Portugal), c. 1880, © Casa-Estúdio Carlos Relvas.
13. Women's woollen socks, Bucos, Cabeceiras de Basto, 2011.
14. Lace cotton stockings, Minho.

Women's work socks
from Northern Portugal

Socks for rural labour needed to be both hardwearing and comfortable. An example of these are the woollen socks and leggings shown in image 13, which come from Bucos (Cabeceiras de Basto), and while they may be in one block colour or patterned, they follow a model that is common throughout the North of Portugal. The heels and toes are the first parts to wear out, but the leg parts can still be worn to protect the legs and can be worn with clogs or even bare feet.

These kinds of socks are made from undyed, finely handspun, 2-ply yarn, which is then knitted in a density of approximately 16 stitches per 5cm (2in). The example shown here has a decorative edge, the technique for which is given on page 93. The shaping of the leg section is achieved through a section of eyelet increases followed by evenly spaced decreases. The increases and decreases are made symmetrically to the left and right of the *revesilho*. These socks follow a very simple pattern, but they are also a perfect example of how raw materials can be optimized and meet functionality, as they gently fit the curve of the leg and stay up when worn.

Women's lace stockings from Minho

When I saw you make stockings
With such lightness and grace
I thought ill of your vanity
But well of your lace[15]

Over a period of time, full lace stockings gradually entered the dress of folk groups throughout the country. However, one hundred years ago, they were less common and were reserved for special occasions only. It appears that the production of this type of stocking – both in the variety and in the complexity of the patterns used – developed more widely in Alto Minho, and led to a thriving trade with Galicia, where they were sold right up to the start of the 20th century.[16] Their survival is due in large measure to the interest in the regional folklore and costumes of Viana do Castelo, although this continues to be threatened by industrially produced garments.

These socks, which are nowadays made from commercially produced white mercerized cotton yarn of variable thicknesses, tend to be knee-high or over-the-knee. Footless models are also common. The more intricate models have lace patterns all over (excluding the sole of the foot and toe), as traditional shoes leave most of the foot uncovered.

The majority of patterns are distributed through vertical sections and composed mostly of eyelets and simple or double decreases. The designs can be very complex, particularly when they are made using very fine thread. Bobbles, where certain stitches are worked in isolation over several rows and then rejoined, are characteristic of such designs. The different patterns are named after nature and everyday life, with names like *pinha/*pine, *concha*/shell, *favo*/honeycomb, *leque*/fan, *espinha*/thorn, *olho*/eye, etc. (image 14).

Pauliteiros de Miranda socks

These men's socks are part of the Pauliteiros de Miranda do Douro dancers' costumes, and date from at least as far back as the early 1930s, which is when the costumes were retrieved or reinvented together with the dance (the pauliteiros).[17] They are made from natural undyed white and dark brown yarn, and decorated with a contrasting horizontal zigzag pattern at the top or down the leg using the French chevron technique. They are knee high and are held up with a garter. As the trousers the dancers wear are short, the socks and their two-toned stripes are clearly visible (images 15 and 17).

Grille or grades socks (Meias de grades) from Bucos

In the village of Bucos, in the municipality of Cabeceiras de Basto, which has connections to the Casa da Lã do Museu das Terras de Basto [the wool hall in the Terras de Basto museum], there is a group of women who continue to make these grades socks. Their name derives from the vertical patterns that are known as grades (grilles). Each grade is made of an odd number of knit stitches, usually 7, 9 or 11, and is then separated by a decorated narrow stripe. The top of the leg is ribbed – known locally as revesilho – and the patterns extend symmetrically down to the heel and toe.

The back of the heel is called the mão-travessa ('hand palm', a name that seems to correspond to the approximate depth of the heel), the triangle formed by the decreases around the sides below the ankles are known as the cunha and the toe is called mates. The leg is approximately 20cm (8in) long (image 16).

Despite their rich decoration, the socks were worn by men rather than women on Sundays under the local traditional leather and wooden clogs. Up until the mid-20th century, they were still produced to order, for sale, as well as for family members. They are made from locally sourced and handspun 2-ply yarn made on a distaff and handheld spindle at a density of approximately 15 stitches per 5cm (2in).

Concha socks (Meias da concha) from northwest Portugal

One of the most unusual examples of Portuguese socks are the meias da concha, as they are known in Mezio, Castro Daire. They are men's work socks from regions where women used to wear socks or stockings with very little decoration. The technique used to make them – known nowadays as mosaic or slip stitch knitting – is little known outside just a few areas in the northwest of the country. Examples that are available come from the villages of Palaçoulo (Miranda do Douro) and the Serra de Montemuro, and the local elderly women continue to produce them to this day. In the Museu de Arte Popular collection there is also a pair described as originating from the Serra da Estrela.

They are made from locally handspun 2-ply yarn in its natural colours. Their name was explained to me by two women from Mezio: the pattern that runs through the fabric is the same pattern as the skin of the local horned vipers [Vipera latastei], which have zigzagged backs that are almost identical to that of the socks. They were made not only for domestic use but also for sale or for exchange with other agricultural products. The oldest examples seen are delicately made and are from the 1960s, held in the collection of the National Museum of Ethnology.

Well worn and heavily darned at the heel, the area of greatest wear, these have a density of 18 stitches per 5cm (2in) (image 18).

15

16

17

18. Meias da concha [Concha socks], Serra de Montemuro, 20th century.
19. Meias dos namorados [Lovers' socks], Serra de Montemuro, 20th century.
20. Meias de pescador [Fishermen's socks], Póvoa de Varzim, 20th century.
21. Woman from Azurara knitting, 1979.

Lovers' socks (Meias dos namorados) from Serra de Montemuro

The *Meias dos Namorados* also come from Mezio, in the Serra de Montemuro. Made from the same undyed natural yarn, they differ in the technique employed to make them and in the specific context of their use.

They are made using a stitch known as *encanastrado*, [entrelac], where two colours are worked individually in opposite directions, forming contrasting squares.

This stitch is not unique to the region as it is also used in socks and pouches in Alentejo (see image 45). In the mid-20th century in Mezio, they were a courting gift made and offered by girls to the boys they liked. By wearing them, and because the cut of the trousers showed off the leg of the sock, a boy was publicly committing to their relationship. The technique for this sock pattern has already been forgotten by local women, but the memory of its use and its symbolism continues. The examples available belong to the collection of the National Museum of Ethnology (image 19).

feature is the brightly coloured horizontal stripes. The central stripe is wider and has geometric or figurative patterns (stars, birds, etc.), and the stripes above and below are usually narrower and textured. The sock narrows gradually towards the foot, which is worked in the usual way. The socks shown in image 20, with narrow stripes that were originally blue but are now faded through use, were acquired in Póvoa de Varzim in 1967 by Sebastian Pessanha and were the inspiration for the leg warmers seen on page 120. They are made of very fine wool (15 stitches per 5cm/2in) which appear to be handspun, and are 42cm (16½in) long.

Azurara, in the parish of Vila do Conde opposite the River Ave, is known as the main production centre for socks and other knitted garments worn by the region's fishermen.

These pieces were domestically produced by women, who would start learning how to make them aged about nine, and were sold in order to supplement the family budget. With experience and using thick yarn, a sock could be completed in about three hours. The raw materials for these were bought ready to use and came from the wool production regions in the countryside (image 21).

Fishermen's socks (Meias de pescador) from Póvoa de Varzim

Fishermen's woollen socks were made all along the coast, however, the most richly decorated examples come from the coastal area north of Porto, between Matosinhos and Viana do Castelo.

Nowadays they are made from very thick wool or synthetic yarn and are sold as tourist memorabilia, but until just a few decades ago, they were still worn by the men of the sea. They are very long socks made from undyed white or brown wool.

The cuff is worked in garter stitch, and their main

Herdsmen's socks (Meias de maioral) from Ribatejo

Interesting detail: It is the peasants themselves who, while in the field watching over the cattle with their crooks under their arms, make their own socks; just as the old ladies from Minho who hold this responsibility for others and who – even while walking – never cast aside their needles. This adoption of a traditionally feminine and time-consuming task by Ribatejo herders, sitting and knitting, next to their herds on the marsh or on the moor is surprising, yet also it is interesting to see how fulfilling this is for them, far from home, making

22. Peasants dancing the fandango, 1950–1960.
23. Girl wearing Serra de Ossa socks, 20th century.

best use of time in a process which alleviates loneliness and makes them independent in terms of clothing.
Alberto Pimentel, 1908[18]

The socks worn by the herdsmen from Ribatejo until the mid-20th century are some of the most interesting examples of Portuguese knitwear and were the subject of a detailed study at the end of the 1970s by Maria Micaela Soares.[19] They were, at least in part, made by the men who wore them, which was very unusual in Portugal, and were considered as workwear. Like Alberto Pimentel, Leite de Vasconcelos also dedicated some lines to them when he described these peasants in an article on the traditions of Estremadura:[20] *In the unoccupied hours while they are watching their cattle, they spend much of their time not only making 'galrichos' (small reed or cane baskets used to carry the fish they catch or buy), wooden pipes and horn spoons, but they also do what used to be considered as women's work – lace-making, knitting, crochet – a little like Hercules who, when dressed as a woman, spent time spinning at the feet of Omphale to make a good impression!*

These knee-high socks were made from very fine white cotton yarn (without the shine of the mercerized cotton used nowadays), and were visible as they were worn with short trousers held up with a lace finished with a silver buckle. Like many Portuguese socks, these herdsmen's socks start with a border of small raised points or picots (see, for example, page 93). This is followed by a wide stripe decorated with columns with a variety of relief motifs created with clustered stitches. The tie is below this bar, and tends to be hidden. The leg is plain, but from top to bottom there is a highly decorative *revesilho* stripe in relief alongside which are the symmetrical stitches required to adjust the sock to the shape of the leg, and two richly worked raised lateral motifs that continue to the foot, which were known as the *árvore* [tree] (image 22). These socks gradually fell from use as the short trousers they were worn with for work were no longer used, and they are now restricted to folk presentations and exhibitions of traditional peasant costume. They were time consuming to make, often taking up to three weeks to complete a single pair. Those produced more recently tend to be finer and lacier. The design of herdsmen's socks is the same as one that has existed since at least the 17th century, with examples found in other countries.

Embroidered socks
from Serra de Ossa

These women's socks that are still produced in Aldeia da Serra (Redondo) (image 23) represent the high point of technical mastery and the motifs used in their design seem to be unique in Europe. There is only a small group of elderly women who still have the skills to make them. As far as they remember, even when they were children, these socks were only worn at Carnival time, and there is no other information about their history or other uses.

It was not uncommon throughout the Alentejo region to find beautiful socks decorated through stranded colour work; however, those from Aldeia da Serra differ in their particular vertically arranged patterns and their predominant use of red and yellow. These socks were mentioned at the end of the 1970s by the authors of the book *Artes e Tradições de Évora e Portalegre* [*Arts and Traditions of Évora and Portalegre*], and were unusually a highlight of an article dedicated to Portugal in 1977 by the French crafts magazine *100 Idées*. The knee-high socks are made using cotton yarn, however, they may have originally been made from wool[21] as Estremoz, a traditional centre of wool production, is just a few kilometres away from Aldeia da Serra, but the women who are still alive are unable to confirm this. The yarn currently used is mercerized cotton no. 12, which has replaced the old matte yarn whose less resistant colours tended to fade after successive washes, which explains in part why there are no earlier examples remaining in the village. The most common motifs, even though examples are relatively rare, are similar to those found in other Portuguese textiles. A flower in a vase is reminiscent of the woven motifs in the aprons from Viana do Castelo, and a rose and its leaves is almost identical to the filet crocheted curtains that still decorate many windows. The flower or eight-pointed star is one of the most common and widespread motifs, and is used in knitting from the peninsula as far back as the 13th century, as seen in the Leonese pillow mentioned in the first chapter. Although red and yellow are the most predominant colours used (image 24), black and white, and blue and white are not uncommon. New York's Metropolitan Museum has a pair of cotton socks of Portuguese origin in its collection that were acquired in 1969. They are worked in blue on black, and their appearance suggests they were made in Serra de Ossa.

These socks are so complex because they are made using two contrasting coloured cotton yarns. Cotton has a much lower elasticity than wool, and requires a very carefully controlled tension so that the design appears smooth without any irregular patches. The motifs only appear after several rounds, so the women follow a knitted swatch until the first repeat of the motif is finished and can be used as reference piece (image 25). The complexity of the design makes it difficult to knit these socks while doing other chores, as we saw was the case for simpler garments.

The socks are created in the usual way, from the reverse side and starting at the leg, using two colours. They require two knitting pins or safety pins – one on each side of the chest – and the thumbs of both hands are used to keep the tension for each thread. The widest area, at the top of the leg, has narrow stripes. This is followed by the motif that goes down the leg, separated occasionally by a different stripe that is decorated with a narrower horizontal motif. Almost imperceptible extra stitches are incorporated to fit the sock to the leg, and these are carefully distributed throughout the design. The foot can be worked in stripes identical to those at the start or, if the socks are intended to be worn with open shoes, they may be more complex, with the pattern continuing down to the instep, and the sole in vertical stripes. The toe is usually striped.

Hats and caps

As shown in Chapter 1, knitted headwear in Portugal has a long history. In their simplest form, hats are technically variations of the toe of a sock, i.e. a knitted tube with sequentially decreasing stitches. Depending on the spacing of these decreases, these hats can take on a conical or even spherical shape (image 26). However, there are many Portuguese traditional caps with even more elaborate forms, with flaps or ear coverings, tassels, pompoms and other decorative elements.

Whaler's beret (*Boina de baleeiro*) from Corvo Island

The traditional berets from Corvo Island were commented on by José Leite de Vasconcelos, who visited in 1924 (image 31). At the time, they were worn by most of the older men, and were the whalers' standard workwear. Some say the Corvo islanders had been taught how to make them by Scottish fishermen, and the same type of beret had been made in Scotland since at least as far back as the 16th century. There are some surviving examples from this period, and the design and production technique appear to have remained unchanged. Although it is not possible to pinpoint exactly when the Corvinos adopted this Scottish beret, it represents one of the most interesting cases of the survival of Portuguese traditional knitwear (image 27).

Originally made from local wool, dyed dark-blue, the berets are nowadays produced in synthetic yarn, but otherwise remain unchanged. The base of the beret is a rim that is decorated on the outside with a narrow colour work motif [*grega*], and on the inside with the owner's name using the same technique. In some cases, the border also has a knitted flap, reinforced with woven fabric. Once complete, the beret is placed in water with a metal ring inside the top to give it its final shape. Finally, a pompom is sewn on top.[22]

Man's cap from São Miguel Island

Little known beyond the Azores, these wool berets from the island of São Miguel are still made by some local artisans, though they are currently only routinely worn by folk groups. There are records of them that date back to the end of the 1830s, when the British travellers Joseph and Henry Bullar described the islanders' dress in *A Winter in the Azores*: *Their headdresses were equally piebald (...) the conical caps of party-coloured worsted, knit by the natives*.[23] In other passages, the Bullars mention that these hats were also common on the islands of Pico, Faial, where they were sold at the fair by elderly women who travelled from Pico for the purpose, and Flores, perhaps with some regional variations but all with the same bright colours and conical shape that had caught the authors' attention. Their book also contains the oldest known image of the São Miguel berets (image 28). It is an engraving made from the authors' drawings that illustrate in detail the various types of Azorean headwear (image 29). Although the engraving is small, it shows the roots of the patterns still used to decorate berets today.

With the conical shape mentioned by the Bullars and measuring approximately 40cm (15¾in) in height, the berets are made with five needles and a medium-thickness yarn. They are started at the rim and are usually edged in a similar fashion to many other traditional knits (see page 93), and are topped with a *berlota* or tassel. In São Miguel in the northeast, the wool used is still prepared and spun locally, but in other regions the yarn is now bought in from other islands or even from the mainland. The variety of colours and patterns described for the oldest berets are almost impossible to find in the earliest photographic records (image 30), and therefore there are unfortunately few known traces left. What have survived until today are those on a white background with graphic motifs and different horizontal stripes in black or dark brown.

28

29

30

Man's cap from Terceira Island

Like those from São Miguel, the berets from Terceira survive only as traditional folk wear and touristic memorabilia. Modern versions are usually crocheted, but in the past, they were more often knitted on five needles. Hugging the skull, they are made with alternate bands of knit and purl, which gives them their characteristic vertical, wavy texture. They are topped with a crocheted string ending in a large tassel (image 32).

Villain's cap (Barrete de vilão) from Madeira

The wool caps from Madeira, also known as villains' caps, ear caps and wool caps [*barretes de vilão, barretes de orelhas, barretes de lã*], continue to be worn in some of the island's more remote areas (image 33). The feature that separates them from most of the other pieces mentioned is the density of the knit, as the yarn used to make them is unusually thick in proportion to the size of the needles used. The wool is still handspun from the local Madeiran Churra sheep. After it has been hand-plied, it has a minimum thickness of 5mm (¼in).

The needles – which are approximately 2.5mm (⅛in) in diameter, are often made from recycled umbrella ribs [*baleias*], and are sometimes bent at one end to form a barbed hook. Together this means that the knit is exceptionally compact and rigid. Traditionally worn only by men, these hats also have two earflaps [*cabeçotes*],which can be pulled down to protect the ears from the cold, or folded upwards where they hold their position. They are made using the short row knitting method (see page 94). After the flaps and the back, which are made using a plain knit stitch, the hat is worked in a circular fashion, gradually narrowing towards the top, which is crowned with a large tassel circled by the final stitches. Its height and shape are just one of many regional variants, with some hats covering just the top of the skull, and others with flaps that were long enough to be fastened with a button under the chin; some hats that were perfectly spherical and others had a bottleneck shape reminiscent of the woven *carapuça* (another kind of headwear) that are also typical of the island (image 34). Although records only date back to the 19th century, their history is probably much longer. According to Luisa Gonçalves,[24] in the past they were likely to have been a domestic task for men, despite the fact that they are almost exclusively made by women nowadays. In more recent decades, these hats have also been made from industrialized, often synthetic yarn, which is smoother and more elastic, and is therefore more suited for the tourist market for which they are produced.

Sweaters

The predecessors of modern sweaters, these knitted tunics were produced at least as far back as the 16th century. The examples that still remain were luxury items – the clothing of kings and princes made of silk using fine needles. The oldest known example, which belongs to the collection of the Museum of Fabrics and Decorative Arts [*Musée des Tissus et des Arts Décoratifs*] in Lyon, is reputed to come from Spain, which was at the time where the finest knitted items were produced. Three centuries later, the knitted sweater had become a common garment and was worn by the working classes of the mainland and islands, although we

31

32

33

Madeira — Costume

34

31. Leite de Vasconcelos on the island of Corvo, flanked by men with berets, 1924.

32. Boys carrying water, Terceira Island, end of the 19th century.

33. Man with beret, Ribeiro Frio, Madeira, 2012.

34. Couple dressed in traditional Madeiran costume, postcard, end of the 19th century.

still don't know how and when this happened. The straight lines of the sweaters and their cut do not greatly differ from the pattern of earlier fabric tunics, but their purpose was now to insulate, made from compact, durable, wool. Images of Portuguese sweaters go back to 1821, with William Combe's image of a Madeiran fisherman wearing a thick woollen sweater (image 35). Subsequently, and thanks to growing interest in regional clothing throughout the 19th century, there were several noteworthy lithograph collections sold separately, and a concurrent proliferation of illustrations of traditionally dressed figures wearing this item of clothing. The oldest collection (the Joubert collection, 1825–1830) shows sweaters worn by the mule drivers [condutores do tojo] from Alcochete, by a donkey-driver and by two fishermen – one from Barreiro and another from Ericeira. In the period between 1840 and 1860 (in the Palhares collection) there are more and more people shown wearing woollen sweaters: cow herders, boatmen, and street vendors in Lisbon, and fishermen and lifeguards from Oporto (image 36). The sweater was now widespread, especially, but not exclusively, in coastal areas. Two particular designs stand out from these images. The most common has a similar shape to the old-fashioned tunics, with a vertical opening over the chest that is secured with two or three ties. Natural white wool seems to be the most commonly used and, as seen in the Joubert collection's engravings and Emílio Biel's photograph of an Afurada fisherman (image 37), the decorative and embroidered elements and alternate use of knit and purl stitches create patterns in relief. The simpler version tends not to be patterned and has a simpler neckline, with sometimes a crew neck or even a roll neck. Both are characterized by their straight fit between the body and sleeves, without any tailoring, and it is this that gives them the characteristic drop shoulders. Made using thread that is fine enough

to be comfortably worn under other clothing, these sweaters are not particularly stretchy, like many other traditional knits when compared with those produced industrially, as their priority was to provide the thermal insulation of wool.

Poveira sweater (Camisola poveira) from Póvoa de Varzim

The Poveira sweater belongs to the family of open-neck sweaters that are made using natural white yarn with embroidered decorations – in this case cross stitch – which was common in several regions in the country. Its survival as a tourist product and a symbol of the popular culture of Póvoa de Varzim is due to an ethnographic campaign begun in the 1930s by António dos Santos Graças. Described as an item of clothing for feast days, it fell into disuse among the fishing community (and the rest of the country) at the end of the 19th century, something locally attributed to the widespread mourning that took place after a terrible shipwreck in 1892.[26] It had already fallen into disuse, when in 1936, in the context of a publicity campaign for popular culture to promote local traditions, Santos Graça reintroduced it to the annals of folkloric costume. There are few traces of Poveira sweaters prior to Santo Graça. However, there is a clear representation in one of the illustrative engravings in the book O Minho Pittoresco (1886), and the Póvoa de Varzim Municipal Ethnography and History Museum also has an interesting set of photographs from the early 20th century (though it does not have any actual examples from the era) (image 38). The embroidered areas are restricted to the chest and the tops of the arms, and the comparatively small motifs are part of the repertoire of popular cross stitch embroidery of the time, such as birds, flowers, Greek motifs, Portuguese coats of arms, and so on. The recreated

35

36

N.º 37.
Pescador do Barreiro e Seixal

37

35. Fisherman with knitted sweater, illustration from *A History of Madeira...* by William Combe, 1821.

36. *Fisherman from Barreiro e Seixal*, lithograph from the Palhares collection (2nd series), 19th century.

37. Fisherman with embroidered woollen sweater, by Emílio Biel, postcard printed in 1904.

38. Fisherman from Póvoa de Varzim, 1910–1915.

39. Frame taken from the film *Ala Arriba*, by Leitão de Barros, 1942.

40. Poveira sweater, mid-20th century.

40|

38|

39|

This sweater was stolen from a Portuguese Fisherman.

The place is Nazare, north of Lisbon...where the boats are painted in Roman stripes and the sweaters are works of art. Helen Harper captures the Portugee Look in a cardigan of Acrilan® acrylic fiber. 34-40. In your favorite color at your favorite store. About $12. Coordinated wool slacks and skirts. 10-16. Chemstrand, New York 1, a Division of Monsanto Chemical Company, makes Acrilan acrylic fiber.

Helen Harper. **Stolen Sweaters made of Acrilan**

ACRILAN
acrylic fiber
CHEMSTRAND

sweater of the 1930s, which was the inspiration for current designs, is made from a thicker yarn that is now more often industrially produced and synthetic. The embroidery is now larger and incorporates nautical motifs such as boats, oars, anchors, ship's wheels and sea creatures, as well as the familiar, traditional Poveira symbols shown in the *The Fishing Boat [O Poveiro]*.[27] In 1942, Leitão de Barros' docudrama film *Ala-Arriba! [Go Upwards!]*, based on Santos Graça's book, brings the peasant sweater to the big screen, making it definitively one of the most iconic designs in the repertoire of Portuguese regional costume (images 39 and 40). The Portuguese fishermen's sweater also attracted attention further afield: in 1962, the North American knitwear brand Helen Harper included several designs in its publicity campaign (image 41). Also in the USA in the early 1980s, the yarn brand Candide published a booklet with instructions on how to knit a Portuguese fisherman's sweater.

Other pieces
Gloves and wrist warmers

Used to protect the hands and wrists from the cold and from manual rural labour, knitted gloves, muffs, cuffs and wrist warmers of wool or flax (image 42) have had several references throughout the country, though there are only a few examples documented in museum collections. Among others are images and examples of wrist warmers (fingerless mittens) from the Trás-os-Montes region (image 44), of straight, woollen tubes from the Serra de Montemuro – delicate flax gloves of the women of Alentejo (image 43), and thick fishermen's mittens from the Algarve.

Purses and pouches

Little is known about these knitted purses, as they tended to be worn under other clothing. They were used to hold money and other small objects, and were made from at least the Middle Ages until the 20th century. They are usually in the form of a knitted tube that is closed at one end, with an opening that can be secured with a tie. The base can be either straight, triangular or rounded. They are often technically identical to the foot of a sock, which is probably the reason why the Portuguese expression *pé-de-meia* [literally, the foot of the sock] is used as a synonym for savings. These knitted purses are rarely mentioned in ethnographic studies, and are different from the better known fabric purses worn outside the clothing (image 45). The most interesting sign of how far these go back is their spread throughout Latin American countries, where, as we have seen, knitting was introduced by the Spanish and Portuguese colonizers. The *monederos* [purses] made and used by indigenous people in Bolivia and Peru, which sometimes take the elaborate form of human and animal figures, are – in their simplest versions – identical to those from the villages of Portugal and Spain. Image 46 shows a Spanish girl in Peru in the late 18th century wearing one of these colourful purses with its characteristic decorative tassel. More common than the purses were the larger, rectangular, white knitted bags that were used until relatively recently throughout the country to carry packed lunches or personal possessions (image 47).

42. Cross-stitch embroidered wool gloves, 19th to 20th century.
43. Cotton gloves, Alentejo, pre-1962.
44. Girl wearing woollen gloves, postcard, Chaves, early 20th century.

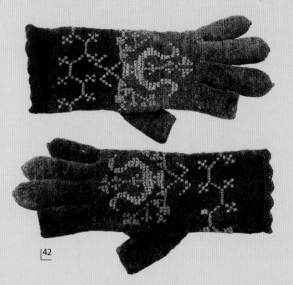

42

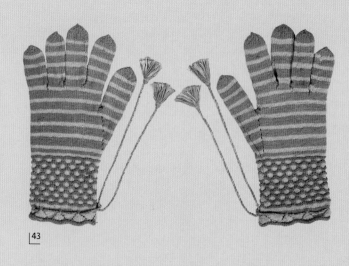

43

44

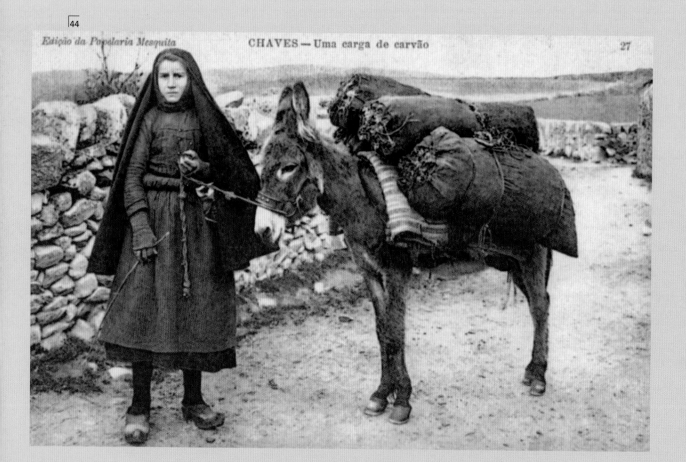

45. Cotton purse, Alentejo (?), 20th century.
46. Spanish woman with purse at the waist and embroidered stockings, Peru, late 18th century.
47. Cotton bag, 20th century.

45

46

47

48. Knitted cotton throw by Maria do Rosário Pires, 20th century.
49. Lace collar made using two needles, Portuguese World Exhibition, 1940.
50. Examples of lace edging, 2012.

Blankets and rugs

Traditional production of small knitted blankets and rugs is always associated with recycling materials. Knitted pieces using strips of fabric from old clothes were common throughout the country, and were identical to those used on the looms to weave the better known rag rugs.Of particular note is the technique that uses these strips of fabric within a basic knitted piece into which they are interwoven; they are called thrummed rugs [tapetes de trapos presos] – see page 95.

Bedspreads

Decorative cotton bedspreads, usually in white or beige, made of knitted strips or squares in different stitches and normally with patterns in relief (such as leaves, bobbles, etc.), are common to this day (image 48), and are made for sale by, among others, the Mogadouro Artisans' Association (Bragança).

Lace edging

Less demanding and easier to learn than other types of lace making, knitted lace was widely used to decorate clothing and linen, and is still made throughout the country. They are known as *rendas por música* (literally 'lace by music'), because they were made and shared using written patterns that use a simple code of O for the loops and X for the stitches (see page 142). This code is the so-called 'music' of the lace and was created to pass the designs from one generation to the next, usually by women who couldn't read or write.

Made using cotton of variable thicknesses, the widest pieces can be time consuming and complex to make. A huge collection of this lace edging can be found in the book *Rendas por Música* [*Lace by Music*] by Maria José Roxo, published in 1986[28] (images 49 and 50).

1. Answer: The lace making needles. Recorded by Manuel Viegas Guerreiro in 1955. *Tecnologia e Tradição*. [*Technology and Tradition*]
2. Vasconcelos, 1938.
3. Letter from a witness transcribed in Vasconcelos, 1975, p. 100.
4. Correia, 1916, pp. 50–52.
5. Vasconcelos, 1938 & 1975.
6. Correia, 1916, pp. 50–52.
7. Vasconcelos, 1996, p. 14.
8. The Castilians, who also use Agave from the Indies, use this very material to make socks, stockings and other garments. Bluteau, 1728.
9. Henriques, 1867, p. 23.
10. Lima, 1903.
11. May, 1939, p. 343.
12. Marreiros, 1995.
13. Vasconcelos, 1938, pp. 442–454.
14. Knitting song. Learned by Maria Isabel Alves as a child, Castelo de Paiva.
15. Traditional picture, 1910s. Vasconcelos, 1996, p. 17.
16. Vasconcelos, 1996.
17. Cf. Correia, 2008.
18. Pimentel, 1908, p. 41.
19. Soares, 1982.
20. Vasconcelos, 1920, p. 50.
21. Artes e Tradições, 1980.
22. The creation of the whaler's beret was partially documented in Gonçalo Tocha's film about the island of Corvo, *É na Terra não É na Lua* [*It's on Earth, not the Moon*].
23. Bullar, 1841, vol. I, p. 21.
24. Gonçalves, 2011.
25. Madahil, 1968.
26. Costa, 1980.
27. Graça, 1932.
28. Roxo, 1986.

48

49

50

Introduction

The materials required for any knitting project are simply yarn and a pair or set of suitable needles. Learning the basic stitches is a quick and simple process, and even more complex techniques used to be taught without written instruction and through imitating the actions of an experienced mother or grandmother.

The longevity and popularity of knitting is precisely because it is such a simple technique for producing garments, both elementary and elaborate, using very few tools and raw materials, and because it can be done while walking or performing other tasks such as watching over the flocks or watching a movie on television.

This chapter is intended as a kind of starter manual, and is directed at people who already know how to knit, or who want to learn to knit in the Portuguese style, which as seen above, is restricted to Portugal and only a few other regions and countries mentioned on page 28. It introduces some of the basic concepts and gives advice for novices, suggesting types of yarn and needles, concepts of tension and density, and it also explains how to accomplish the stitches and techniques necessary to complete the patterns in the following chapter.

Materials

Yarn

The texture of a knitted piece largely depends on the structure and composition of the yarn being used. Identifying and getting to know the characteristics of different yarns is crucial in order to predict the final effect. Yarns differ according to the composition of the fibres, and the thickness and texture they acquire from the processes of spinning and plying.

Fibres

Yarns are normally described as natural (those obtained from animals and plants), artificial (those with a natural basis but subject to chemical processing) and synthetic (created from petroleum by-products). They can be grouped into three main compositional groups:

Protein fibres: these include all natural animal fibres, both wool and those from other species like silk (taken from the cocoons of silk worms). Recently developed fibres, such as those made from soya bean or milk protein, are also included in this group.

Cellulose fibres: these include all natural vegetable fibres such as cotton, flax, hemp, jute, pita, and cellulose-based fibres such as viscose, Tencel and bamboo.

Synthetic fibres: these are created via chemical processes using petroleum by-products and include Nylon, polyester, acrylic, etc.

Until the end of the 19th century, the variety of textiles was composed exclusively of natural fibres of vegetable and animal origin. Synthetic fibres were invented and developed soon after, and they gradually became more popular, not only in the clothing industry, but also in terms of yarn for domestic production. However, in recent years, increased cultural and environmental awareness raised by artisan knitters has meant that the unique characteristics of natural fibres are again being used. Wool is considered the best raw material for knitting due to its numerous qualities – which include the fact that it is permeable to air and also hydrophilic – meaning that it will continue to heat the body even when it is wet, yet allows the body to breathe even when the temperature rises; it is biodegradable and can be obtained from local sources almost anywhere, and it is resistant and elastic and comes in different colours, tones and textures.

Different fibres create knitted fabrics that behave and wear differently: cellulose-based fibres and silk are lighter and, in general, smoother to the touch, while fibres of animal origin produce naturally warmer fabrics. Synthetic fabrics are usually cheaper than natural fibres and became increasingly common from the 1970s, not only because of their cost, but also because they had innovative colours and textures and were machine washable. Today, the best yarns only include synthetic fibres in small proportions. Mixtures like this are, in some cases, advantageous; for example, yarn for socks tends to be made from 75% wool and 25% nylon, which makes them more hard-wearing, even though the feel of completely natural fibre is far more pleasant than any synthetic or mixed yarn.

Thickness and ply

It is not only the composition, but also the structure of the thread that determines the texture and behaviour of knitted fabrics. The thickness of the yarn is the most obvious factor, and reference books and sites usually use classifications on a scale of 0 to 6, where 0 or lace weight corresponds to the finest thread, usually used for shawls and scarves (see the Caninhas shawl on page 128), and 6 (super bulky) is used for the thickest yarns on the market (see the scarf 'by music', page 104).

What is most important to take into account when choosing the thickness of yarn for a project is the following: the thicker the yarn, the less it will produce, i.e., the smaller the surface area. This means that an average 50g skein will have many more metres of yarn if it is thinner rather than thicker. It follows therefore that more balls are needed to make a heavy sweater than one that is lighter, and that the final weight of the former will be considerably more than the latter.

The spinning process that forms the yarn consists of applying a continuous tension to the fibres and gradually stretching them towards the manual or mechanical spindle (image 1).

These fibres are pre-prepared using two alternative techniques: either combing or carding (images 2 and 3). In short, the combing process aligns the fibres so they are parallel to each other and the resulting yarn is smooth, shiny and compact with no nap, and therefore less likely to pill. This is known as worsted. For the carding process the fibres are prepared using carders, either manual or mechanical, and are organized in various directions. In hand spinning, the carders form sections of fibres that are arranged perpendicularly to the thread that creates them, and these are traditionally known as *pastas*, *panadas* or *betas*. Carded yarns are naturally less regular and tend to be fluffier, warmer and more matte than those that are combed. When the yarn is spun, it can create woollen fabrics whose final appearance is only revealed after the first wash, after which they become softer and denser as the fibres expand and realign.

1. Spinning wool with a manual spindle, São João, Pico, 2012.
2. Combing the wool. Duas Igrejas, Miranda do Douro, 2012.
3. Carding the wool. Ribeiro Frio, Madeira, 2012.

Yarn, whether worsted or carded is then generally plied, i.e., composed of two or more single threads wound around each other in the opposite direction to that of their individual twist. This can easily be seen by looking at a commercial thread and lightly stretching it between the fingers. When they are twisted, the threads become more resistant and balanced, and produce a more regular knit. Knitwear made using single ply yarn tends to have a slightly skewed appearance that comes from the tension the yarn itself gives to the fabric.

Needles

The needles are the only indispensable tool for knitting. Until recently, the needles available on the market were almost all made of metal or plastic, but needles made from bamboo and other wood are now increasingly popular for many pieces (image 4). In the second chapter, we saw how the knitting needles traditionally used in Portugal have a hook at one end. However, nowadays most needles on sale are exactly the same as those used in other countries. The needles are numbered on a scale that corresponds to their diameter in millimetres.

The diameter of the needles you use for any given project depends on the thickness of the yarn required. It is this that determines the consistency of the fabric: for any yarn, the finer the needles, the denser and less elastic the knit will be. As each knitter has their own tension, the choice of needles should also take this factor into account: for example, if you tend to knit quite tightly, you should choose slightly thicker needles – 0.5 or 1mm greater in diameter – than those suggested on the label.

Knitting needles can be divided into three main categories, as described below.

Single-pointed needles
Two needles of equal length – normally 25–35cm (9¾–13¾in) long, with or without a hook, and with a stop at the other end to prevent the stiches from dropping off; used for knitting flat pieces.

Double-pointed needles
A set of five needles of equal length, for working in the round. The lengths depend on the diameter of the pieces being made. Portuguese needles are hooked at one end and have a point at the other. They are used for knitting seamless tubular pieces such as stockings, caps and gloves.

Circular needles
A pair of needles consisting of two rigid tips joined to each other by a flexible cable of varying size. They are used to knit both flat and tubular pieces. Circular needles are usually used for larger pieces, as the stitches can be spread along the cable. For tubular pieces, the total length of the needles (tips and cable) has to be less than that of the perimeter of the final piece.

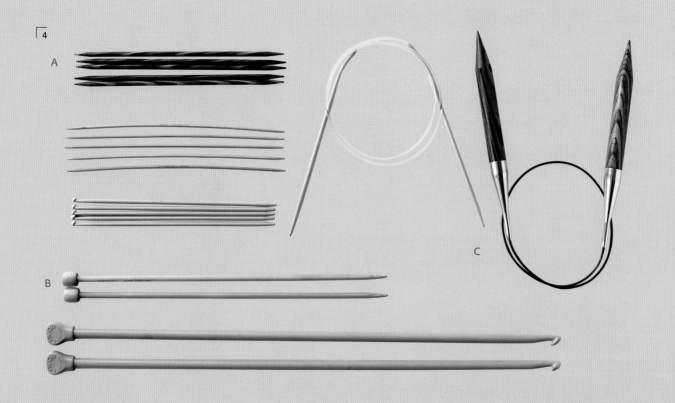

A

C

B

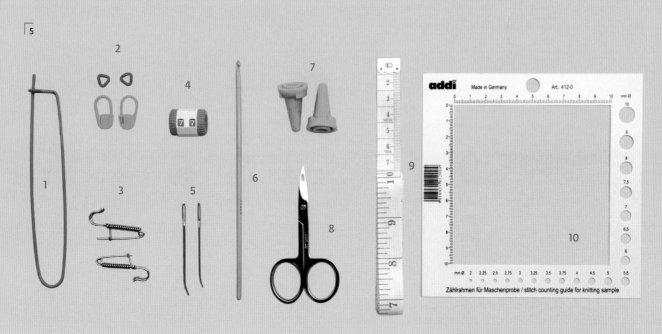

2

4

7

1

3

5

6

8

9

10

addi   Made in Germany   Art.: 412-0

mm Ø

Zählrahmen für Maschenprobe / stitch counting guide for knitting sample

A Double-pointed needles **B** Single-pointed needles **C** Circular needles
1 Stitch holder **2** Stitch markers **3** Knitting pin **4** Stitch counter **5** Sewing needles for knits **6** Crochet hook
7 Tip protectors **8** Scissors **9** Tape measure **10** Needle calibrator with stitch counter

Accessories

In addition to the needles, there is a set of basic accessories (image 5) that are useful to have to hand, either for finishing or to help at other stages. The most important are the following:

Knitting pin

As referred to previously, the knitting hook or pin is widely used in Portugal to support the yarn. Some knitters consider it indispensable as the pin prevents the yarn rubbing against the neck. It is usually affixed to the left-hand side between the chest and shoulder.

Crochet hook

When knitting with standard needles, a slim crochet hook can be a very useful aid to pick up dropped stitches. This hook can also be used for several kinds of finishes and seams.

Tapestry needles

Blunt tapestry needles are used for most finishes. They are very useful for weaving in loose yarn ends.

Tape measure

This is essential to measure the swatch samples and to calculate the density of the knit.

Scissors

Just as for any other textile project, a pair of small scissors should always be on hand to cut the yarn when necessary.

Other useful tools

Stitch markers

These are small rings or locks made of plastic or other materials, which can be positioned on the needle or hung from the knitted fabric to mark certain key stitches in the work, for example, the position for making increases or decreases.

Tip protectors

These prevent the knitted fabric from slipping off the needles in breaks between knitting sessions.

Stitch counter

These record the total number of stitches you have worked. The numbers displayed are advanced manually at the end of each row.

Pin for securing knits

Made of metal or plastic, these help to save knitted pieces that have been temporarily set aside, to be worked on at a later stage.

Needle calibrator with stitch counter

A perforated plate with holes with diameters that correspond to the most common widths of knitting needles. This makes it possible to quickly identify the needle size. It covers a 10cm (4in) range to measure swatch samples and calculate stitch density.

Interpreting labels

The labels of commercial knitting yarns include important information and should be kept (for example within the ball of yarn) for later reference:

1 Batch identification: there are often numerous small differences in colour between batches, so all balls of yarn used for a single job should come from the same batch.

2 Colour identification

3 Recommended swatch sample and density: the average number of stitches and rows needed for a 10 x 10cm (4 x 4in) sample.

4 Washing instructions

5 Recommended needles: the needle size number for the yarn to achieve a balanced density.

6 Weight: the weight of the skein.

7 Composition: identifying the fibres the yarn is made of and its respective percentage.

8 Length: the number of metres of yarn in each skein.

Knitting

Unlike woven fabrics, which are created on a loom of taut threads (the warp) between which the filling threads are interlaced using a shuttle (the weft), knitted fabrics are formed from a continuous thread, forming units on the needles – the stitches – which in turn form rows or rounds. Each visible loop on a needle is a stitch. A row is complete once all the stitches have passed from one needle to the other. Once completed, each stitch depends on the one to its right and left, and also on that above and below it. This is why even a tiny hole will grow so quickly: by breaking the structure of the fabric, each thread that is undone causes adjacent threads to unravel as well.

The knitting needles are held in each hand, and are gently held between the tips of the thumb and forefinger. The yarn is passed behind the neck or through the pin, usually from left to right, and then passes to the right hand. Tension is applied by the yarn being wrapped around one of the fingers of the same hand, usually the middle finger or the thumb.

Tension, density and swatch samples

Forming a stitch consists of passing the yarn through a loop and in that movement, creating a new stitch. How the thread is worked initially determines whether it is a knit or a purl stitch. These are the two basic knitting stitches that really are just one, as a purl is the reverse of knit and vice versa.

In two-needle knitting, a row consists of sequentially working through all the stitches on the left-hand needle and passing the new stitches onto the right-hand needle. At the end of each row, the needles are exchanged and the process continues. This means that a row that is worked on the right side of the piece follows one that is done on the reverse side, and then by another one on the right side and so on. In tubular knitting this is done using circular needles or two-point needles, and the piece is worked in a spiral, thus always being on the right side, or the reverse, of the piece. This is why the term a 'round' is used for what in flat pieces is known as a 'row'.

The yarn tension (gauge) while making the piece determines its texture and density. Saying that a certain knitter has a tight or loose stitch means that the person applies greater or lesser pressure than that which is desirable. Too much tension creates a compact and rigid fabric, and not enough tension creates an open, irregular fabric. A well-balanced tension comes through practice and by using the right sized needles, but it is natural to have slight variations from person to person.

The density of the knit is measured according to the number of stitches and rows required for a given area (usually a 10cm^2/4in^2 piece) with a given yarn. This varies not only with the thickness of the needles used, but also with the tension of the knit itself. Knitting patterns usually indicate the correct tension for the knit. It is important to follow these suggestions, as the final dimensions of the piece will depend on them. To check the density, a small swatch sample should be made with a few more stitches and rows than those set out in the pattern. When completed, the swatch should be carefully ironed and the corners secured with pins (for example to the ironing board) without stretching it. Then, with the aid of a stitch counter or tape measure, the swatch should be measured to find how many stitches and rows correspond to a square of the suggested size. If more stitches than those suggested are required, the swatch should be remade using slightly thinner needles, and if there are fewer needed, then slightly thicker needles should be used for the project. Needles that produce a swatch of the correct size are the ones that should be used for the final project.

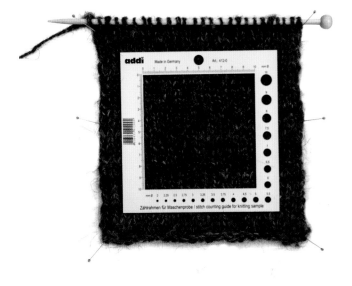

Starting to knit

The first step of any knitted piece is to cast on the required number of stitches. In addition to the methods shown here, there are numerous other ways of casting on, which give results that differ in appearance, firmness and elasticity. When a very supple piece is required, it is better to cast on the stitches using a slightly thicker needle than the one to be used for the rest of the piece.

Single casting on

Single casting on produces a light and delicate edge. As its name suggests, it is simple to do, despite the fact that the first row is more difficult to do perfectly. This is done using a single needle. This method of casting on is often used when there is a need to add further stitches at the start or the end of a row.

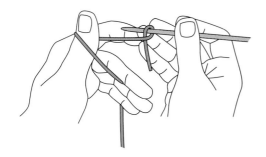

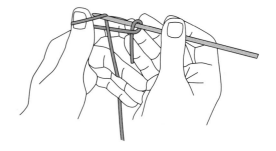

1. With the needle in the right hand, the yarn is passed around it from front to back, thus creating the first stitch. With the yarn held firmly between the right-hand fingers, pass it in turn around the thumb of the left hand.

2. Insert the needle into this loop from bottom to top, in order to create a new loop.

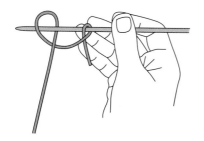

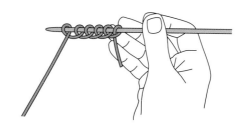

3. Release the thumb from the loop and adjust it on the needle.

4. Repeat steps 2 and 3 as many times as necessary.

Portuguese-style casting on

This method of casting on is the most commonly used in Portugal and creates a firm, stretchy edge. The yarn is passed behind the neck or through a pin and uses a single needle. It requires two lengths of yarn; so before starting, unwind a length of yarn equivalent to that of approximately three turns around the needle per stitch, and start casting on from this point. For projects where elasticity is essential, as in the case of socks and stockings, it is better to cast on using a needle that is thicker than that required for the rest of the piece.

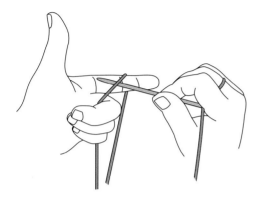

1. With the yarn in the correct position, it is passed around the left forefinger from back to front, leaving the long end of yarn between the fingers of the left hand.

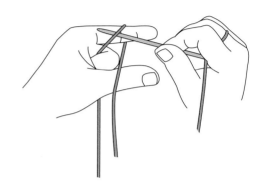

2. With the needle in the right hand, insert the needle tip under the back of the forefinger from right to left.

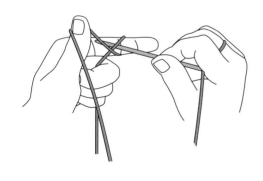

3. With the thumb, pass the yarn over the needle tip.

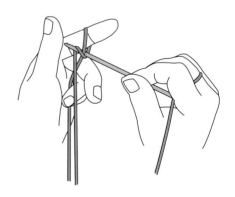

4. Then using the needle tip, pull the yarn back through the loop which is around the forefinger, from left to right.

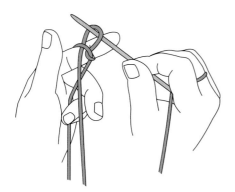

5. Form a stitch on the needle in the right hand.

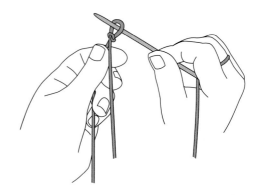

6. Remove the forefinger from the loop of yarn and carefully adjust the stitch onto the needle without making it too tight.

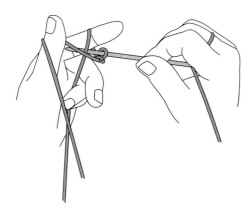

7. Repeat steps 1 to 6 as many times as necessary.

Purl and knit

The names of the two main stitches used for knitting in Portuguese are *liga* and *meia* [purl and knit] – and they come from the garments that bear the same names. *Liga*, literally meaning 'tie', comes from the ties or garters used to hold up socks, and *meia* means socks or stockings, which for centuries were the most common knitted garments.

Purl stitch

Purl stitch is the most simple. For flat pieces made using two needles, when all the stitches are in purl, the result is purl or garter stitch, which in the north of the country is usually known as *manta de gato* [cat blanket]. This stitch, which is characterized by horizontal wavy lines, produces a flat yet voluminous knit and is often used for scarves, throws and baby clothes.

Purl stitches are worked from right to left, with the yarn to the front of the piece.

How to create a piece in purl:

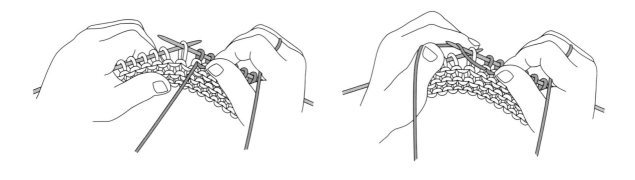

1. Insert the tip of the right-hand needle from right to left into the first stitch of the left-hand needle.

2. Use the left thumb to pass the yarn over the tip of the right-hand needle.

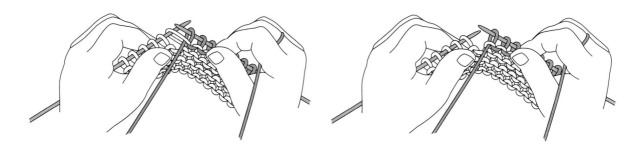

3. With the right-hand needle, lift and remove the yarn from the inside of the stitch, creating a new stitch on this needle.

4. Release the original stitch from the left-hand needle.

Knit stitch

Knit stitch is used in conjunction with purl stitch to create what is known as stocking (US stockinette) stitch – or in Portuguese the *ponto de meia*. For a flat piece, this stitch is achieved by using knit stitch for every row on the right side, and purl for the reverse. Knit stitch is the most widely used in all knitting patterns.

If all the rows are worked in knit stitch, this will produce a garter stitch, identical to that mentioned above but with a greater density. As it is simpler and faster to use purl than knit stitches in the Portuguese method, it is relatively uncommon to use knit stitch for this purpose.

In the most common method of Portuguese knitting, knit stitches are worked from left to right, with the yarn always behind the piece.

How to work knit stitch:

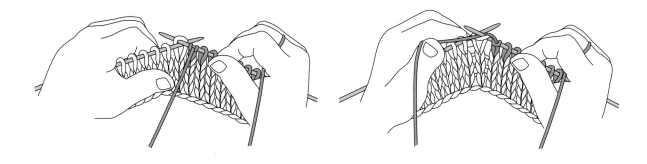

1. Insert the tip of the right-hand needle from left to right into the first stitch of the left-hand needle.

2. Use the left thumb to pass the yarn over the tip of the right-hand needle.

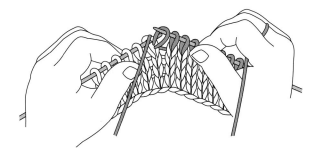

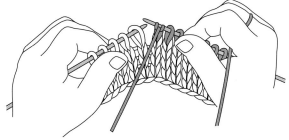

3. Re-insert the right tip of the needle into the stitch, but this time from right to left, thus forming a new stitch on this needle.

4. Release the original stitch from the left-hand needle.

An alternative knit stitch method

There is an unusual, alternative method of working knit stitches from the reverse of the piece, which is simple to do. It requires using a hooked needle – a needle with a crochet hook on one end and a knitting point on the other end – in the right hand. In this method, the needles do not change hands at the end of each row, and the knitted row is worked from left to right, using a technique very similar to that of Tunisian crochet.

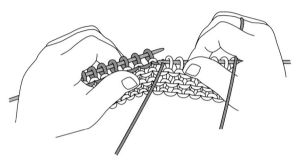

1. Using the right-hand needle, pull the yarn through the first stitch on the same needle, from left to right, thereby releasing the original stitch.

2. This creates a new stitch on the right-hand needle.

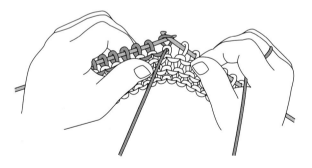

3. The newly-created stitch is then passed to the left-hand needle, passing the tip of this needle through the stitch from right to left (this detail is essential so that the knit is correctly placed on the needle).

4. Release the stitch from the right-hand needle.

Rib stitch

Rib stitch is formed by alternating a vertically parallel knit row with a purl row, forming contrasting rows. It is a very supple stitch, often used for socks, sweaters and hats. The most common variations of rib stitch are 1/1, alternating between one purl stitch and one knit stitch, and 2/2, alternating between two purl stitches and two knit stitches, and they are in general made using needles that are one or two sizes smaller than those used for the rest of the piece. The 1/1 rib works where the number of stitches is a multiple of 2, and 2/2 where the number of stitches is a multiple of 4. It is also possible to make irregular rib stitches, for example, 1 purl to 3 knit stitches, but the elasticity of the piece reduces as the number of consecutive same stitches increases.

Rib stitch 2/2:

First row:

1. Work two purl stitches.

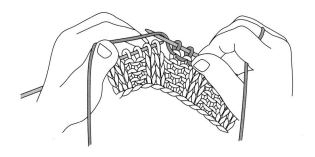 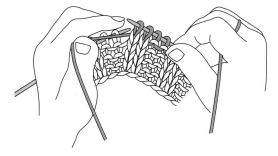

2. With the left thumb, pass the yarn behind the right-hand needle so that it is in the correct position to continue with knit stitches.

3. Work two knit stitches.

4. With the left thumb, bring the yarn to the front of the right-hand needle so that it is in the correct position to continue with purl stitches.

5. Repeat steps 1 to 4 until the end of the row.

Following rows:

Continue, working purl stitches in purl, and knit stitches in knit.

Stitches and techniques

There is an almost endless array of knitting stitches and techniques. Just changing and combining knit and purl stitches creates a huge variety of patterns and results. When these are combined with the other main techniques (increases, decreases and slip stitches), the potential for different effects is vast. This book presents only a small selection of stitches that are indispensable for the projects shown in the following chapter. The aim is to explain the different steps for each using the Portuguese knitting technique with the yarn passed around the neck or shoulder.

Flat and circular knitting

For knits worked with two needles, all the stitches are cast on to one needle and the rows are worked as above, alternating between the right and the reverse sides of the piece, and exchanging the needles between hands at the end of each row. In the first row, following casting on, the first stitch is the same as the last one to be cast on. Circular knits, however, use four needles to cast on (or the entire length of a set of circular needles). The piece is made in a spiral, where the first stitch to be worked is the same as the first stitch that was cast on, thus closing the circle that forms the base of the piece.

Circular knitting has two major advantages over flat knits: first, it avoids many of the seams and finishes required by two-needle knitting, and second, it also makes it possible to work stocking stitch in purl, which is much simpler and faster than having to switch rows of purl and knit as is necessary in a flat knit. In Portugal, traditional circular knitted garments (socks, hats and so on.) are almost always worked on the reverse side, for both efficiency and convenience.

Knitting with five needles

Knitting with circular needles

Circular needles can be used as a substitute for the five needles in mid to large tubular pieces. It is, however, essential to take into account the total length of the circular needles (including the needles and the cable), which must be shorter than the edge of the piece to be worked.

1. The stitches should be cast on and distributed evenly over the whole length from one end to the other.

2. Introduce a marker for the last stitch cast on to mark the end/beginning of the round.

3. Form a circle with the needles, and turn the base of the stitches carefully inwards so that the work does not get twisted.

4. The tip with the first stitches should be held in the left hand and the tip with the yarn should be held in the right hand. Create the first stitch, making sure it is tight enough to avoid a space between the stitches.

5. Work the following stitches. After the first round, move the marker to the right-hand needle and start the next row in the same way.

The stitches are cast on to four needles, with the fifth needle left empty. Less experienced knitters can choose to cast on the stitches on a normal needle and then distribute them over the four needles.

1. Cast on approximately a quarter of the total number of stitches to each needle.

2. Place a marker on the fourth needle next to the last stitch cast on, to mark the end/beginning of each round.

3. Form a square with the needles, turning the base of the stitches carefully inwards so the piece does not get twisted.

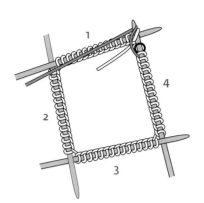

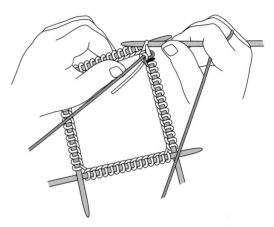

4. With the fourth needle in the right hand and the first needle in the left hand, work the first stitch of the first needle. This stitch needs to be tight in order to avoid any gap between the stitches.

5. Release the fourth needle and work the rest of the stitches from the first needle with the free needle.

6. Always work through the stitches of the following needle with the needle that has just been released. Once the first round has been completed, move the marker to the needle on the right and start the next round in the same way.

Some advice:

– If the first three or four stitches of the first round are worked with both the working yarn and the yarn tail together, this will be interwoven within the piece and means that weaving in the loose end will not be necessary.

– The following technique should be used if the point where one needle passes to another is visible in the piece: once all the stitches of one needle have been worked, work a further two stitches to the right-hand needle before starting to use the empty needle again.

Selvedges

Selvedges are the lateral margins of pieces made using two needles. To ensure that the selvedges are regular, which facilitates sewing (page 91) and picking up (page 92), a few simple but essential techniques can be used, including the following:

Stocking stitch

For every row:

1. Pass the first stitch onto the right-hand needle without working it, taking this stitch as if you were to purl on the purl rows and knit on the knit rows.

2. Work the remaining stitches.

Garter stitch

For every row:

1. Slip the first stitch onto the right-hand needle without working it, taking it as if it were to purl.

2. Work all the stitches except for the last.

3. Work the last stitch as a knit stitch.

Knitting in two colours

Jacquard

Jacquard is the name commonly given to the technique of knitting with different coloured yarns in the same row to create designs and patterns. This technique has been used on the Iberian Peninsula since at least the 13th century, and can be seen in some of the traditional pieces that were looked at in the previous chapter. Some of the most beautiful and complicated of these are the embroidered stockings, known as *bordadas*, made in the Serra de Ossa (see page 47). In Portugal, jacquard usually uses no more than two different colours in each row, and one of the threads is pulled through the reverse side while the other colour is being worked.

The Portuguese method of knitting adapts perfectly to the jacquard technique. Two knitting pins are used in the process, one in the usual position on the left shoulder and the other placed symmetrically on the right shoulder. The yarns are also worked symmetrically, one in the usual position, with one of the fingers of the right hand giving it even tension, and the other in the left hand. The most technical aspect of jacquard is to achieve a regular, supple fabric so that the stitches are neither too loose nor too tight on the reverse of the fabric, but this difficulty is easily overcome with practice.

Working position: with each colour change, use the thumb of the right hand to gently secure the yarn being worked, preventing it from pulling or becoming too loose.

Aspects to bear in mind:

- The fine yarn that comes from carded wool is most recommended for this kind of work.

- Soft, shiny threads are less suitable as it is more difficult to maintain a regular tension in the knit.

- Smaller patterns, with shorter sequences of stitches in the same colour, are easier than those where the same colour is used for more than four or five stitches.

- Circular knitting is an ideal technique for jacquard: the pieces are made from the reverse side, always in purl, making it easy to control the tension of both threads.

- Whenever work is stopped temporarily, the yarn should be put back onto the pin on the same side as it was before, as any accidental change will cause the colours to become irregular.

- In two-needle knitting, the yarn should be swapped from one pin to another at the end of each row, while in circular knitting they should remain in the original position.

Jacquard pattern technique – front and back.

Slip stitch

Another two-colour technique involves using only one colour per row, slipping, without knitting the stitches of the other colour. The unworked stitches are stretched up on the right side of the piece until they are needed, which is generally one or two rows above. This technique is very simple, but it is more limited than jacquard in terms of the patterns that can be made. However, it produces a more elastic, finer fabric than jacquard. It is traditionally used in some villages in the northeast of Portugal, and is used in the patterns on page 134 (Concha Socks) and page 114 (Cuffs).

Examples of patterns made using the slipped stitch technique – from the front and back.

For flat pieces made with only two needles, it is important to bear in mind the following:

– The first stitch of each row is always slipped, regardless of the pattern.

– The last stitch of each row is always worked, regardless of the pattern.

– In the rows of knit, the slipped stitches are worked purlwise.

Decreases

A decrease, as the name indicates, is a reduction in the width of a knitted piece that corresponds to the removal of one or more stitches. For stocking stitch, decreases are visible on the right side of the piece and, depending on the technique used, are right slanting (purl two together) or left slanting (slip slip purl). Decreases are used when a piece needs to be narrowed gradually – for example, on the toe of a sock or the sleeve of a sweater – but are also an integral part of various decorative stitches. For the latter, decreases are normally compensated for by an identical number of increases, so that the proportions of the piece stay the same.

Although many traditional fabrics use only the right-slanting decrease (purl two together), it is worth mastering at least one other decrease technique that leans to the left. This is because many pieces require symmetrical decreases, or example on both sides of a neckline, which look much better if equal on both sides.

The decreases shown here are always done in purl, from the reverse side of the pieces.

Right slanting – purl two together (p2tog)

Purling two together simply means working two stitches at the same time:

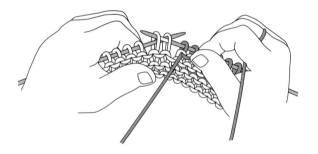

1. Insert the tip of the right-hand needle from right to left into the first two stitches of the left-hand needle.

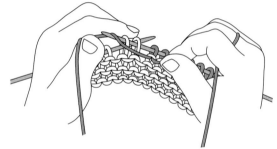

2. Use the left thumb to pass the yarn over the tip of the right-hand needle.

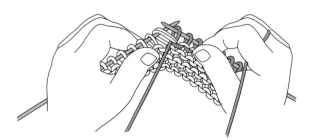

3. With the right-hand needle, remove the yarn from the stitches, thus forming one new stitch on this needle.

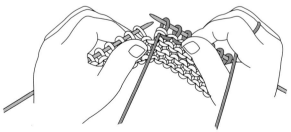

4. Release the original stitches from the left-hand needle.

Left slanting – slip slip purl (ssp)

To make a left-slanting decrease without the knit becoming twisted, the piece must be in the correct position before starting. This detail means that the slip slip purl decrease takes a little longer to do than purling two together:

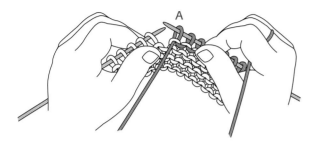

1. Work a purl stitch – stitch A.

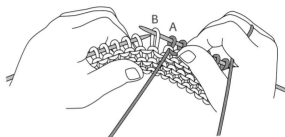

2. With the right-hand needle, take the first stitch from the left-hand needle without working it – stitch B.

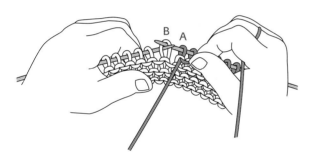

3. Put this stitch back on the left-hand needle, but in the reverse position (so the stitch is oriented to the right side, the opposite of all the others).

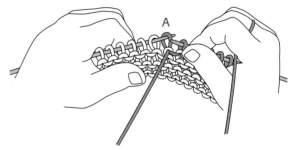

4. Replace stitch A onto the left-hand needle.

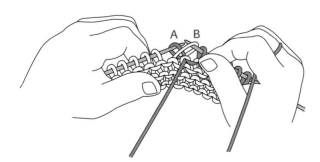

5. Using the right-hand needle, slip stitch B over stitch A.

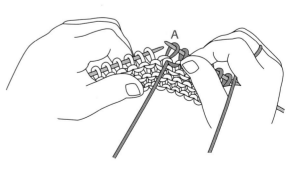

6. Then slip stitch A again onto the right-hand needle.

Increases

Increases are the opposite of decreases. They are used to widen a knit and mean creating new stitches. Among the many types of increase, the two most important are yarn over increases and loop (make 1) increases.

Both techniques shown here are done using purl, from the reverse side of the pieces.

Yarn over increase

Yarn over increases are sometimes known in Portugal as *ajourado*, and create a small opening under the new stitch. They are commonly used in lace making:

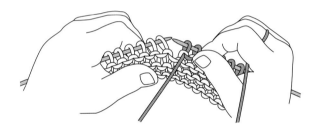

1. Work up to the desired point.

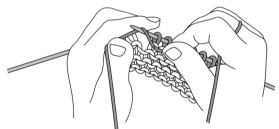

2. Use the left thumb to pass the yarn over the tip of the right-hand needle from front to back.

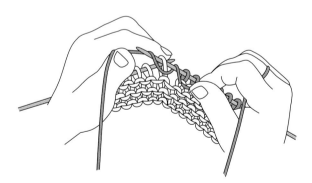

3. Form a loop of yarn over the needle that can be worked as a normal stitch. Work the following stitch as normal.

Loop increase (make 1)

This creates a new stitch between two that already exist. One of the simplest ways of doing this is to cast on a new stitch on the right-hand needle using the single casting-on method (page 75).

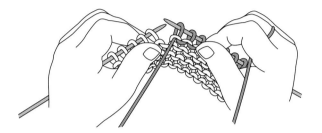

1. Work up to the desired point.

2. With the thumb, form a loop with the yarn on the right needle.

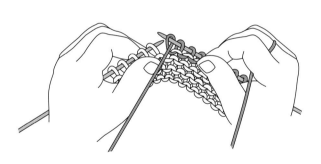

3. Pull the yarn to adjust the new stitch to the needle.

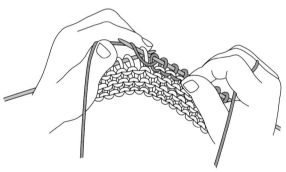

4. Complete the following stitch as normal.

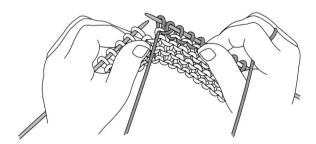

5. The visible increase is between the stitches.

Casting off

Casting off is the last row of a knitted piece, the point at which all the stitches are released from the needle without the piece unravelling. Casting off must not pull on the yarn, as otherwise it will not have the required elasticity. A good way of ensuring the elasticity of the knit is to cast off with a needle that is one or two sizes larger than that used for the rest of the piece. The following technique is one of the most simple.

Casting off in purl

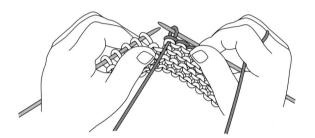

1. Work a stitch in purl.

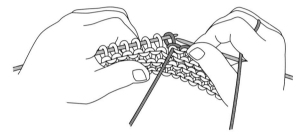

2. Put the stitch back on the left-hand needle.

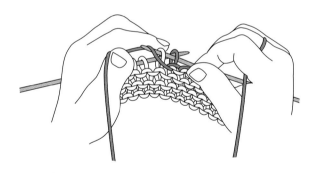

3. Work two stitches together (the one that has already been worked and the next one) in purl.

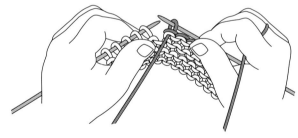

4. Repeat steps 2 and 3 up to the of the row.

5. Cut the yarn, slip it through the last stitch and adjust.

6. Weave the end of the yarn in under the stitches on the reverse side of the piece using a tapestry needle.

Casting off in knit

Proceed as for casting off in purl, but work all the stitches in knit.

Casting off two pieces together (three-needle cast-off)

To join two pieces from the top, casting off can be done on both simultaneously. This job is easier to accomplish with a hooked knitting needle or crochet needle, which should be of the same thickness as the needles used for the rest of the piece. To ensure elasticity, the casting off should be done with care and should not pull on the yarn.

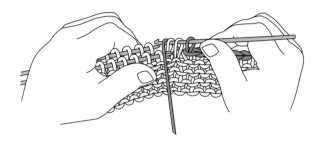

1. Align both pieces right sides together, and work the first stitch on each of the needles together.

2. Repeat with the next pair of stitches and slip the second stitch through the first leaving just one stitch on the right needle.

3. Repeat step 2 to the end of the row.

4. Cut the yarn, passing it through the last stitch and pulling it gently.

5. Cast off the last stitch using a tapestry needle.

Sewing

One of the easiest ways to join the selvedges of two pieces of knitting is to sew them from the back using a crochet needle or hooked knitting needle. The seams should always be made so as not to compromise the elasticity of the knit, and the stitches should not be overly tight. The yarn used should be the same as that used for the rest of the piece.

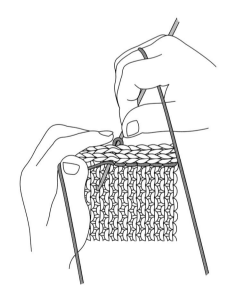

1. Insert the crochet needle under the first stitch of both selvedges and pull the yarn to form an initial stitch on the needle.

2. Repeat for the following stitches, pulling the yarn through the selvedge stitches and then through the stitch on the needle.

3. Repeat step 2 up to the end of the row.

Picking up

Picking up stitches consists of casting on stitches from the edge of a piece. The task becomes simple if the selvedge stitches are worked as previously indicated (see page 83). This is a key element in sock making.

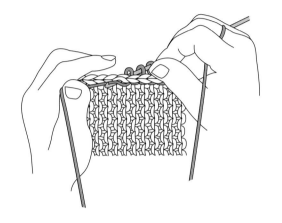

1. From the reverse side, insert the tip of the needle under the two threads of the first selvedge stitch.

2. Pass the yarn over the needle tip and pull it through the selvedge stitch, thereby forming a new stitch on the needle.

3. Repeat steps 1 and 2 for the remaining selvedge stitches.

Joining yarn

Knots should be avoided at all costs. If the yarn breaks or a new skein is needed, the best way to join it is to twist one around the other for approximately 10cm (4in) and then work the two together over four or five stitches.

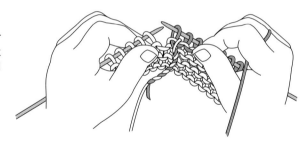

Faggot stitch

Mate e laço, literally meaning 'loop and decrease', is the popular name for a simple stitch that is widely used in traditional Portuguese knitting. It alternates between purling two together (see page 86) and a yarn over (see page 88). It can be used in a single row to create a series of small openings, sometimes used as eyelets for laces or ribbons, or in successive rows to create a lacy stitch. It should be worked with an even number of stitches.

Method:

One yarn over, one purl two together. Repeat to the end of the row.

Picot edging

Based on single casting on and faggot stitching, this decorative edging has been used since the 19th century to edge socks and other traditional pieces. It can be used both for flat knitting as well as circular pieces, but always uses an even number of stitches. It is particularly recommended for pieces that require a fine yarn, and it is easier with patterns using Portuguese double-pointed needles (with a hook at one end). Like most other circular knits, it is worked from the reverse side in purl.

Method (for circular pieces):

1. Cast on the required number of stitches over the four needles using the single casting-on technique (see Single casting on, page 75, and Knitting with five needles, page 82).

2. Work four rounds in purl.

3. One round in faggot stitch. (One yarn over, one purl two together, repeat to end of row.)

4. Work four rounds in purl.

5. Fold the edge over to the faggot stitch, and use the left-hand needle to carefully align them. The stitches from this needle will now be worked together with those from the faggot stitch, thereby closing the hem, as follows:

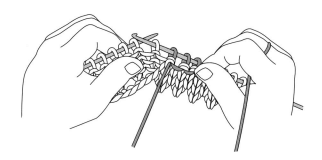

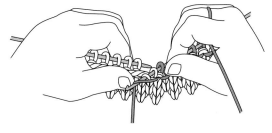

6. Slip the first stitch from the left-hand needle to the right-hand needle without working it

7. Insert the tip of the right-hand needle into the base of the first stitch from casting on.

8. Pass the yarn over the right-hand needle and bring it back through the two stitches (the cast-on stitch and that on the left-hand needle).

9. Repeat steps 6 to 8 with the following stitches until the end of the round.

Variation for hookless needles:

Follow steps 1 to 7.

8. Place the casting-on stitch onto the left-hand needle, followed by the slipped stitch.

9. Work the 2 stitches together in purl.

10. Repeat steps 6 to 9 to the end of the row.

Short rows

The short row technique makes it possible to create curves and other shapes in knitted fabrics. This technique is for example often used for the traditional shepherd caps from Madeira to shape the distinctive earflaps (see the Villain's Cap, page 99), and also for the heels of almost all traditional Portuguese socks. The technique consists of making a return at key points in the rows before completing them, meaning that certain parts of the fabric are longer than others.

Method 1 (used for Villain's Cap):

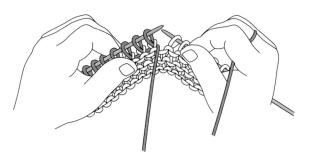 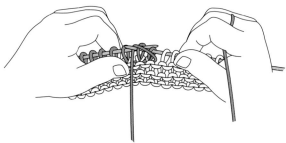

1. Work the row up to the desired point.

2. Return back along the piece.

3. Slip the first stitch onto the right-hand needle without working it, and continue as normal with the remaining stitches.

Method 2 (alternative):

1. Work the row up to the desired point and then slip the next stitch onto the right-hand needle, without working it.

2. Return back along the piece, taking care to pass the yarn to the front after the stitch, rather than behind it.

3. Slip the first stitch onto the right-hand needle (this stitch will be wrapped with the yarn) and then continue as normal with the remaining stitches.

4. In the following row, the wrapped stitch is worked together with the loop around it.

Thrumming

The base of this technique is a simple knitted fabric that incorporates small strips of fabric into the knit. It is used to make blankets and rugs and needs needles that are relatively narrow in relation to the yarn chosen, so the rags are secured firmly within the knit. As seen in the second chapter (page 62), this is a technique associated with reusing both yarn and fabric. The rags are interwoven in the knit at regular intervals; for example: 3 purl stitches, 1 purl stitch with rag, 3 purl stitches, and so on.

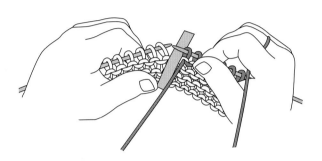

1. For a row on the reverse side, work in purl up to the desired point. Place the rag alongside the next stitch to be worked so that it is centred (half to the front of the piece, and half to the back).

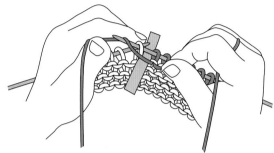

2. Work the following stitch in purl.

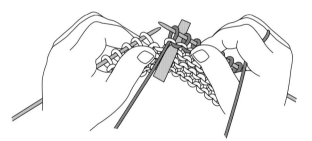

3. The strip will be secured between the stitches.

4. Fold the strip over, so that both ends are to the right side of the piece and are the same length.

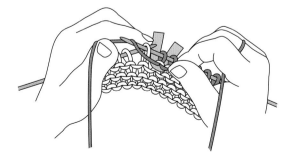

5. Work the following stitch in purl.

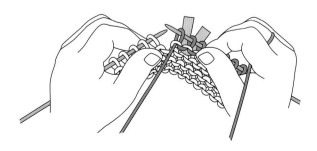

6. The strip is now 'trapped' within the stitches and secure.

PATTERNS

Abbreviations and other terms used

The following patterns are based on traditional Portuguese designs. Some – such as the Villain's Cap or the Concha Socks, seek to replicate the originals as faithfully as possible. Others – like the Caninhas Shawl and the Serra de Ossa Leggings – are based on traditional techniques and motifs that have been adapted.

The traditional methods used to make these were born of necessity, and required a profound understanding of the raw materials. With rare exceptions, they have been passed on orally, learned through imitation or through trial and error, without any recourse to written instruction. Translating the methodology of a piece of knitwear into numbers and abbreviations inevitably leads to a less organic approach than that achieved through observing the fabric to understand its structure. However, it makes it possible to interpret into an intelligible form pieces that would otherwise be overly complicated for beginners.

The techniques needed to make the patterns have been set out in the previous chapter, and the patterns indicate at the start which techniques are needed.

It is advisable to read the instructions from start to finish before embarking on any of the projects, even though some sections may seem confusing before you reach this stage of the piece.

Tension (gauge) considerations

If you want to use a different yarn from that suggested for a given project, always knit a tension swatch first to test it. You should try to find yarn that has an identical composition, and that will result in a tension swatch that is as similar as possible (with an identical number of stitches and rows for the area indicated) to the original.

...	Asterisks are used to mark the beginning and end of an instruction that should be repeated (for example: *p1, k1*). The number of repetitions necessary is always indicated next (for example: Repeat from * to* until end of row.).
(... sts)	Number of stitches that should be on the needles after completing the instruction before the brackets. This enables you to check that the instruction has been followed correctly.
m1	make one (loop) increase (see page 89)
yo	yarn over increase (see page 88)
ssp	slip slip purl decrease (see page 87)
p	purl (for example: p3 - work 3 purl stitches)
k	knit (for example: k4 - work 4 knit stiches)
p2tog	purl two together decrease (see page 86)
slp	slip purlwise (for example: sl1p – slip one stitch purlwise)
slk	slip knitwise (for example: sl1k - slip one stitch knitwise)

Villain's Cap (Barrete de vilão)

The Villain's Cap (see page 53) owes its characteristic shape to the fact that it is made using a thicker than average yarn in proportion to the needles used, and to the technique of short rows which are used here to shape the earflaps. In this version, the hat – which was originally made from a rough Madeiran sheep's wool, employs a softer handspun yarn. To obtain the required thickness, work with two strands of yarn held together.

●●○○○

MATERIALS AND TOOLS
150g Retrosaria Bucos (100% wool) mixed colour

5.5mm (US 9, UK 5) circular needles (optional)
Double-pointed 5.5mm (US 9, UK 5) needles
Tapestry needle

TECHNIQUES USED
Short rows (page 94), five needle knitting (page 82) and purling two together (page 86)

NOTES
The entire hat is worked in purl, with the exception of the small front strip that rests on the forehead. The piece is made using two strands of yarn held together.

INSTRUCTIONS

Cast on 41 sts using the Portuguese method of casting on, with two strands of yarn held together.
Row 1: sl1p, working all the sts in purl.
Row 2: sl1p, p4, turn the work.
Row 3: sl1p, p4, turn the work.
Row 4: sl1p, p5, turn the work.
Row 5: sl1p, p5, turn the work.
Row 6: row sl1p, p6, turn the work.
Row 7: row sl1p, p6, turn the work.
Row 8: sl1p, p7, turn the work.
Row 9: sl1p, p7, turn the work.
Row 10: sl1p, p8, turn the work.

Row 11: sl1p, p8, turn the work.
Row 12: sl1p, p9, turn the work.
Row 13: sl1p, p9, turn the work.
Row 14: sl1p, p10, turn the work.
Row 15: row sl1p, p10, turn the work.
Row 16: row sl1p, p11, turn the work.
Row 17: sl1p, p11, turn the work.
Row 18: sl1p, p12, turn the work.
Row 19: sl1p, p12, turn the work.
Row 20: sl1p, work all the sts in purl (41 sts).
Row 21: sl1p, p4, turn the work.
Row 22: sl1p, p4.Turn the work.

Row 23: sl1p, p5, turn the work.
Row 24: sl1p, p5, turn the work.
Row 25: sl1p, p6, turn the work.
Row 26: sl1p, p6, turn the work.
Row 27: sl1p, p7, turn the work.
Row 28: sl1p, p7, turn the work.
Row 29: sl1p, p8, turn the work.
Row 30: sl1p, p8, turn the work.
Row 31: sl1p, p9, turn the work.
Row 32: sl1p, p9, turn the work.
Row 33: sl1p, p10, turn the work.
Row 34: sl1p, p10, turn the work.
Row 35: sl1p, p11, turn the work.
Row 36: sl1p, p11, turn the work.
Row 37: sl1p, p12, turn the work.
Row 38: sl1p, p12, turn the work.
Row 39: sl1p, work all the sts in purl (41 sts).
Row 40: sl1p, p6, turn the work.
Row 41: sl1p, p6, turn the work.
Row 42: sl1p, p9, turn the work.
Row 43: sl1p, p9, turn the work.
Row 44: sl1p, p12, turn the work.
Row 45: sl1p, p12, turn the work.
Row 46: sl1p, working all the sts in purl (41 st).
Row 47: sl1p, p6, turn the work.
Row 48: sl1p, p6, turn the work.
Row 49: sl1p, p9, turn the work.
Row 50: sl1p, p9, turn the work.
Row 51: sl1p, p12.Turn the work.
Row 52: sl1p, p12, turn the work.
Row 53: sl1p, work all the sts in purl (41 sts).
Row 54: sl1p, p8, turn the work.
Row 55: sl1p, p8, turn the work.
Row 56: sl1p, p14, turn the work.
Row 57: sl1p, p14, turn the work.
Row 58: sl1p, work all the sts in purl (41 sts).
Row 59: sl1p, p8, turn the work.
Row 60: sl1p, p8, turn the work.
Row 61: sl1p, p14, turn the work.
Row 62: sl1p, p14, turn the work.
At this point, both earflaps are completed. The next step is to increase the sts for the front of the cap, and this is done using a circular knitting technique from the wrong side.
The new sts will join the front section between the two earflaps.
Using the single casting-on method and without cutting the yarn, increase 15 sts.
Place a marker on the needle to mark the end/beginning of the round (56 sts).

Taking care to ensure that the newly cast-on sts do not get twisted, work a complete return in purl.
Next round: p38, k18.
Next round: k3, then work in purl until end of round.
Next round: p38, k18.
Next round: k3, then work in purl until end of round.
From this point on, the rest of the piece is done in purl.
Next 7 rounds: purl.
Next round: *1p2, p2tog*, repeat from * to * until end of round (52 sts).
Next 2 rounds: purl.
Next round: *p6, p2tog, p7, p2tog*, repeat from * to * until a stitch before end of round, p1 (46 sts).
Next 2 rounds: purl.
Next round: p4, p2tog *p6, p2tog, p5, p2tog*, repeat from * to * until 2 sts before end of round, p2 (40 sts).
Next 2 rounds: purl.
Next round: p3, p2tog, p4, p2tog, p5, p2tog, p4, p2tog, p5, p2tog, p4, p2tog, p3 (34 sts).
Next 2 rounds: purl.
Next round: p2tog, p4, p2tog, p3, p2tog, p4, p2tog, p3, p2tog, p4, p2tog, p4 (28 sts).
Next 2 rounds: purl.
Next round: p2, p2tog, p3, p2tog, p3, p2tog, p3, p2tog, p3, p2tog, p2, p2tog (22 sts).
Next 2 rounds: purl.
Next round: p1, p2tog, p2, p2tog, p2, p2tog, p2, p2tog, p2, p2tog, p1. p2tog (16 sts).
Next 2 rounds: purl.
Next round: p2tog eight times (8 sts).
Cut the yarn leaving a length of approximately 30cm (11¾in), and with the tapestry needle, pass the yarn through the 8 remaining sts, without drawing the top of the hat too tightly. Make a large pompom approximately 7cm (2¾in) in diameter. Place the pompom on the opening at the top of the hat, and secure it using the yarn that was passed through the last 8 sts.

FINISHING
Cast off the yarn ends, weaving them through the stitches on the reverse side.

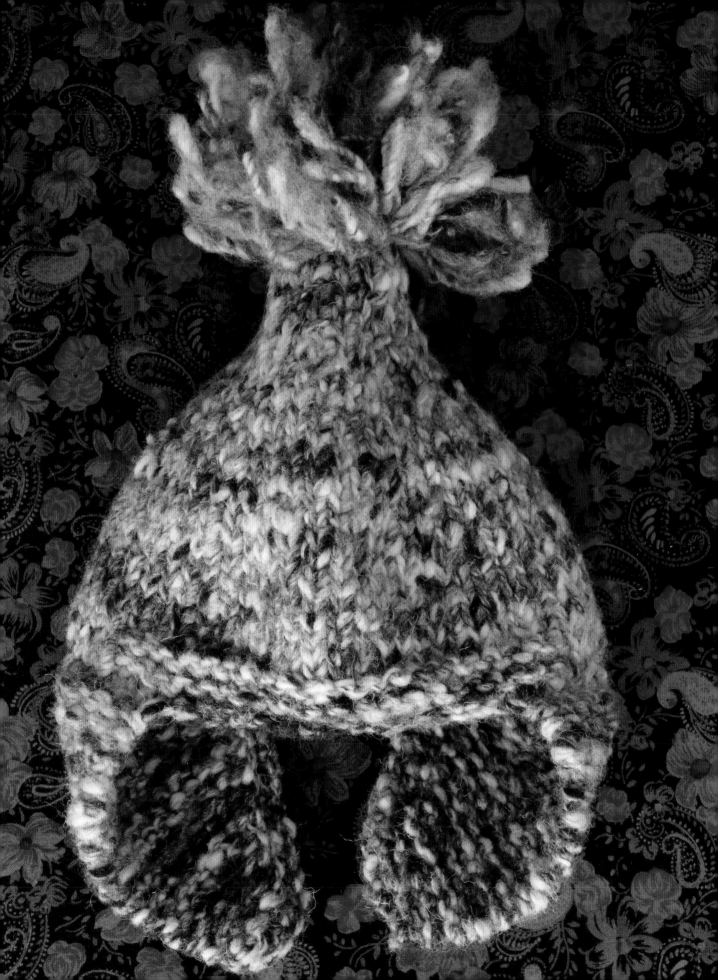

Algibeirinha Pouch

These knitted pouches have been used for centuries on the Iberian Peninsula, yet despite this, are relatively little known. Worn by both men and women, they were used to carry money and other small objects. The pouches here have been made using crochet cotton no.12 and 2mm (US 0, UK 14) needles. They can be worn around the neck, hung from a long strap.

●●●○○

MATERIAL
Yarn: Limol Mercerized Cotton no. 12
Blue pouch: 5g of colour 56 (A) and 5g of colour 22 (B)
Red pouch: 5g of colour 37 (A) and 5g of colour linen (B)

2mm (US 0, UK 14) double-pointed needles
Stitch marker
Tapestry needle

TENSION (GAUGE)
4.5 stitches and 6 rows in a 1cm (⅜in) square

TECHNIQUES USED
Purling two together (page 86) and yarn overs (page 88)

INSTRUCTIONS

Using colour A, cast on 45 sts evenly distributed between the four needles. Place a marker on the needle to mark the end/start of the round.
Round 1: purl.
Round 2: knit.
Rounds 3 and 4: purl.
For the following round, you need to make small openings through which the strap of the pouch will pass:
Round 5: *p2, yo, p3tog, yo*, repeat from * to * until the end of the round.
Rounds 6 and 7: purl.
Round 8: p2tog, work remaining sts in knit until end of round (44 sts).
The rest of the piece is now worked in purl. The yarn with the colour that is not being worked should not be cut, but instead passed through the reverse side of the piece to be used when required later.
Next rounds: work 2 rounds using colour B, then 2 rounds using colour A. Repeat until you have completed eleven stripes in colour B.
Check the number of sts on each needle – you should have 11. If necessary, redistribute the sts over the four needles so they are equally distributed.
Remove the stitch marker.
The next stage is to narrow the pouch using decreases, which are made on the last sts of each needle as follows:
With colour A always:
Next round: *work all sts from the left-hand needle apart from the final two. Work the last 2 sts from the left-hand needle together and slip the resulting stitch onto the empty

needle, which is now the new right-hand needle*. Repeat from * to * until there are only 2 sts left on each needle.

Cut the yarn leaving a length of approximately 1.5m (1⅔yd), and with the tapestry needle, pass the yarn through the remaining 8 sts, pulling it tight to close the piece.

FINISHING

With the remaining yarn and using the tapestry needle, make a small tassel for the bottom of the pouch.

Cast off the yarn ends, weaving them through the stitches on the reverse side.

Make a strap of approximately 80cm (31½in) long, either by making a braid or a finger cord, and pass it through the openings at the top of the pouch, finishing with a knot.

Lacy Scarf

This scarf is very simple to make, and is a good starting point to practise decreases and yarnovers. It is based on one of the many patterns in the repertoire of what are known as *rendas por música* – literally, 'lace by music' – (see page 62) but, as it uses a thick woollen yarn instead of the usual much finer cotton, the result is something quite different. The scarf is made using purl stitch, and the lower edge is decorated with a leaf pattern that is repeated every ten rows.

●○○○○

MATERIALS AND TOOLS
300g (3 balls) Rosários 4
Bulky Light (100% wool)
colour 01

7mm (US 10½/11, UK 2)
needles
Tapestry needle

TENSION (GAUGE)
12 stitches x 20 rows in a
10cm (4in) square

TECHNIQUES USED
Purling two together (page
86) and yarnover (page 88)

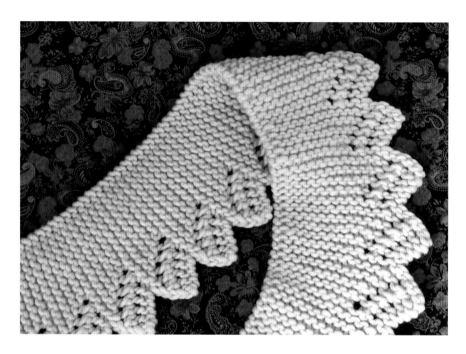

INSTRUCTIONS
Cast on 14 sts.
Pattern:
Row 1: sl1p, p9, yo, p2tog, yo, p2 (15 sts).
Rows 2, 4, 6 and 8: sl1p, work all sts in purl.
Row 3: sl1p, p10, yo, p2tog, yo, p2 (16 sts).
Row 5: sl1p, p11, yo, p2tog, yo, p2 (17 sts).
Row 7: sl1p, p12, yo, p2tog, yo, p2 (18 sts).
Row 9: sl1p, p13, yo, p2tog, yo, p2 (19 sts).
Row 10: cast off 5 sts and work the rest in purl (14 sts).
Repeat the pattern until the end of the third ball or until the scarf has reached the desired length, finishing the last repetition on the 9th row.
Cast off all sts.

FINISHING
Cast off the yarn ends, weaving them through the stitches on the reverse side.

Rag Mat

In several areas of the country, old strips of fabric were used as a raw material, both for weaving, creating the well-known rag blankets [*mantas de trapo*], and for making rugs and other knitted pieces. The same method for this piece, which can also be used as a mat for hot dishes, can be used to make larger squares for place mats, pillow covers, rugs and so on.

●○○○○

MATERIALS AND TOOLS
Approximately 75g of fine cotton fabric

4mm (US 6, UK 8) needles
Tapestry needle

FABRIC PREPARATION
Cut the fabric into approximately 1cm (⅜in) wide strips that are as long as possible. Carefully tie the strips to each other and form a ball. Those familiar with the basics of spinning may use a spindle to twist the fabric strip before knitting, as this will make it sturdier.

TENSION (GAUGE)
18 stitches and 34 rows in a 10cm (4in) square

TECHNIQUES USED
Make one increase (see page 89) and slip slip purl (see page 87).

INSTRUCTIONS
This square mat is made starting from one corner, and is finished at the opposite corner. In the first stage, the piece increases the number of sts progressively until it has reached the desired width, as follows:
Cast on 3 sts.
Row 1: p1, m1, p1, m1, p1 (5 sts).
Row 2 and all even-numbered rows following: all sts in purl.
Row 3: p1, m1, p3, m1, p1 (7 sts).
Row 5: p1, m1, p5, m1, p1 (9 sts).

Following rows: continue to increase the number of sts in the same way, i.e., m1 following the first st and m1 immediately before last st in the odd-numbered rows, to obtain a total of 49 sts.
Even rows: purl.
In the second half of the square, the number of sts is gradually reduced until there are three again:
Row 47: p1, p2tog, p43, p2tog, p1.
Row 48 and all even numbered rows following: all sts in purl.

Following rows: continue to decrease the number of sts in the same way, i.e., p2tog following the first st and p2tog immediately before the last st in the odd-numbered rows, until there are only 5 sts remaining.
Even rows: purl.
Next row: p1, p3tog, p1.
Cast off.

FINISHING
Weave in the yarn ends, working them through the stitches on the reverse side.

Mirandês Bag

This small bag, worn over the shoulder or around the neck, is made from handspun natural white and brown wool. The pattern, worked on the wrong side almost entirely in purl, is inspired by the *mantas de crivo*, a fine-knit kind of shawl, made from hand-woven fabric in the region of Miranda do Douro. The bag has a simple cotton fabric lining.

●●●○○

MATERIALS AND TOOLS
120g Retrosaria Mirandesa (100% wool) in white and 60g in brown

6mm (US 10, UK 4) double-pointed needles (or 40cm/15¾in long circular needles)
Stitch marker
Tapestry needle
A rectangle of cotton fabric approximately 52 x 26cm (20½ x 10¼in)
Leather strap approximately 2 x 120cm (¾ x 47¼in)
Sewing needle and thread

TENSION (GAUGE)
16 stitches and 17.5 rows in a 10cm (4in) square

TECHNIQUES USED
Knitting in jacquard (page 84) and casting off two pieces together (page 91)

PATTERN: USE CHART A (PAGE 148)

INSTRUCTIONS
Using white wool, cast on 80 sts evenly between the four needles. Place a marker on the needle to mark the end/start of the round.
Round 1: purl.
Next rounds: follow Chart A, working in purl, until you have completed it twice (41 rounds).
Next rounds: follow the pattern, completing only the first three rows. Cut the brown wool, leaving approximately 10cm (4in) for the casting off.
Next round: using white wool, knit.
Cast off the two sides of the bag in purl using three needles.

FINISHING
Weave in the yarn ends, working them through the stitches on the reverse side. Adjust the fabric size to that of the bag. Fold the fabric in half, right sides together, and sew up the sides. Sew the lining to the inside of the bag. Using the brown wool, make two tassels for the bottom corners of the bag. Sew the strap to the bag.

Thrum Rug

This small rug, which could also be used as a blanket or throw, is made using the traditional technique of weaving small strips of fabric into a purl knit fabric. With rag rugs, the knit is only visible from the reverse side, which is why this project is suggested for upcycling leftover yarn from other projects. The strips of fabric should ideally be cut on the bias to stop them from fraying.

●○○○○

MATERIALS AND TOOLS
150g Katia Gales (85% wool, 15% polyamide) colour 61
Around 250 fabric strips of approximately 3 x 7cm (1¼ x 2¾in)

4.5mm (US 7, UK 7) needles
Narrow sewing needle

TENSION (GAUGE)
10 stitches and 16 rows in a 5cm (2in) square

TECHNIQUES USED
Rag rugs (page 95)

NOTE
For each row, the first stitch is worked in purl and the last is worked in knit.

INSTRUCTIONS
Cast on 83 sts.
Row 1: purl.
Pattern:
Row 2: sl1p, p2, *p1 with rag, p3*, repeat from * to * until 3 sts before end of row, p2, k1.
Rows 3–5: purl.
Row 6: sl1p, *p1 with rag, p3*, repeat from * to * until 1 st before end of row, k1.
Rows 7–9: purl.

Following rows: repeat the pattern until approximately 4m (4½yd) of yarn is left on the ball.
Next row: purl.
Cast off all the sts.

FINISHING
Weave in the yarn ends, working them through the stitches on the reverse side.

Minderica Cowl

The traditional woven woollen blankets from Minde offer almost unlimited patterns for fans of jacquard. The motifs for this cowl were inspired by an old blanket and have been adapted to the colours and texture of Beiroa wool, made from the wool of Bordaleira Serra da Estrela sheep.

●●●○○

MATERIALS AND TOOLS

Yarn: Retrosaria Beiroa (100% wool):
50g in colour 685 (anthracite), 10g in colour 675 (grey), 10g in 401 (natural white), 10g in colour 515 (yellow), 10g in colour 729 (electric blue), 10g in colour 567 (strong red)

3.5mm (US 4, UK 9/10) 60cm (23½in) circular needles 20cm (7¾in), or a set of double-pointed 3.5mm/20cm (7¾in) needles
4mm (US 6, UK 8) 60cm (23½in) circular needles, or a set of double-pointed 4mm (US 6, UK 8) 20cm (7¾in) needles
Stitch marker
Tapestry needle

TENSION (GAUGE)

24 stitches x 27 rows in a 10cm (4in) square

TECHNIQUES USED

Knitting with circular needles (page 82), pointed edging (page 93), make one increase (page 89), knitting in jacquard (page 84), purling two together (page 86) and casting off in purl (page 90)

PATTERN: USE CHART B (PAGE 148)

INSTRUCTIONS

Using the 3.5mm (US 4, UK 9/10) needles and colour 685 (dark blue) wool, cast on 148 sts using the single casting-on method (page 75), and equally distribute them between the four needles, or along the length of the circular needles. Place a marker on the needle to mark the end/start of the round and make the edging as described on page 93, but with just 3 rounds in purl, before and after the round in faggot stitch, instead of the usual four.

Next round: work a round in knit and, using the make one increase method, make 12 sts evenly distributed along the round (160 sts).

Next round: using the 4mm (US 6, UK 8) needles, work in purl, following Chart B (a total of 48 rounds). The ends of the coloured yarn that are being introduced should remain loose (without knots) and will be woven in at the end.

Next round: using colour 685, purl.

Next round: using 3.5mm (US 4, UK 9/10) needles, work a round in knit, purling two together twelve times at regular intervals along the round (148 sts).

The piece is finished off with the same symmetrical picot edge as at the start, which is done as follows:

Next 4 rounds: purl.

Next round: faggot stitch.

Next 3 rounds: purl.

The casting off can be done in two ways. The simplest manner is to cast off all the sts in purl and close the edge by sewing it to the inside of the piece with a suitable needle and the yarn used for the rest of the piece. The second manner, which is slightly more complex, involves casting off the sts that are on the needle, together with the first of the four rounds in purl from the edging (which are taken from the reverse side), using a method that is very similar to that used to close the edge at the start.

FINISHING

Weave in the yarn ends, working them through the stitches on the reverse side.

Montemuro Cuffs

These fingerless mittens are worked in two colours using a traditional technique from the northeast of Portugal that is still practised today in some villages in the Serra de Montemuro (see page 80). The pattern is one of several still in use in making men's socks. The small lacy border at the top is made by alternating between purling two together and yarnovers. They are made using handspun wool in natural white and dark brown, and are made in a circular knit in purl, from the reverse side.

●●●○○

MATERIALS AND TOOLS
30g Retrosaria Bucos fine white yarn
30g Retrosaria Bucos fine brown yarn

Five 2.5mm (US 1.5, UK 12/13) double-pointed needles
Stitch marker
Tapestry needle

TENSION (GAUGE)
17 stitches and 28 rows in a 5cm (2in) square

TECHNIQUES USED
Knitting with five needles (page 82), pointed edging (page 93), purling two together (page 86), yarn over (page 88), slip stitches (page 85) and casting off in purl (page 90)

INSTRUCTIONS
With white wool, cast on 60 sts evenly (page 75) between four needles. Place a marker on the needle to mark the end/start of the round and make the picot edging as set out in the instructions on page 93, but with 5 rounds in purl, before and after the round in faggot stitch, instead of the usual 4 rounds.
Round 1: purl.
Rounds 2–4: *yo, p2tog*, repeat from * to * until you have completed three rounds (60 sts).
Rounds 5 and 6: purl.
Now start the section that uses the two colours:
Pattern:
Rounds 1 and 2: using brown yarn, *p3, sl1p*, repeat from * to * until end.

Rounds 3 and 4: using white yarn, p1, sl1p, *p3, sl1p*, repeat from * to * until two sts before end, p2.
Next rounds: repeat these 4 rounds another eighteen times and finish by repeating the first 2 rounds once again.
The piece is finished with an edge that is folded to the reverse side in a line formed by a round in knit:
Next 6 rounds: using white wool, purl.
Next round: knit.
Next 4 rounds: purl.
Casting off can be done in two ways. The simplest method is to cast off all the sts in purl and finish the edge by sewing it to the reverse of the piece with a suitable needle and the yarn used for the piece. The second method, which is slightly

more complex, involves casting off the sts that are on the needle together with those from the second of the six rounds in purl from the edge (which are from the reverse side), using a process that is very similar to that used to finish the edge at the start of the piece.

FINISHING

Weave in the yarn ends, working them through the stitches from the reverse.

Repeat for the pair.

Minderica Sleeves

Woollen cuffs are a versatile accessory. They can be worn over the hands as a substitute for gloves, and can also be used to warm children's arms and legs on a cold day. The patterns and colour scheme for these were inspired by a traditional throw from Minde and work perfectly with jacquard. The cuffs are worked from the reverse side in purl, with a ribbed strip at each end.

●●●○○

MATERIALS AND TOOLS

Jamieson's of Shetland Spindrift yarn (100% wool):
25g in colour 101 (Natural Black), 10g in colour 462 (Ginger), 5g in colour 870 (Cocoa), 5g in colour 246 (Wren), 5g in colour 1160 (Scotch Broom), 5g in colour 243 (Storm), 5g in colour 640 (Stonehenge), 5g in colour 104 (Natural White)

Five 2.5mm (US 1.5, UK 12/13) double-pointed needles
3mm (US 2/3, UK 11) double-pointed needles
Stitch marker
Tapestry needle

TENSION (GAUGE)
16 stitches and 17 rows in a 5cm (2in) square

TECHNIQUES USED
Knitting with five needles (page 82), jacquard (page 84) and casting off (page 90)

PATTERN: USE CHART C (PAGE 148)

INSTRUCTIONS
Using the 2.5mm (US 1.5, UK 12/13) needles and colour 101 (Natural Black), cast on 72 sts evenly between four needles. Place a marker on the needle to mark the end/start of the round.
Rounds 1–15: work in 2/2 ribbing (*p2, k2*, repeat from * to * until end of round).
Round 16: using 3mm (US 2/3, UK 11) needles, purl.
Next rounds: follow Chart C. The ends of the coloured yarn that are being introduced should be left loose and will be woven in at the end.

Next round: using colour 101, purl.
Next 15 rounds: using 2.5mm (US 1.5, UK 12/13) needles, work in rib stitch 2/2 (*p2, k2*, repeat from * to * until end of round). Cast off all the yarn as follows: purl sts in purl, and knit those in knit.

FINISHING
Weave in the yarn ends, working them through the stitches on the reverse side.

Pillow

Based on a very simple technique, the attraction of this design is in the characteristics of the yarn used, which create an unusual finish, as it has long filaments. The wool comes from the Churra Galega Mirandesa breed of sheep. After completion, the piece is carded, which makes it much fluffier and softer than the original appearance.

●○○○○

MATERIALS AND TOOLS
Yarn: Retrosaria Mirandesa 2 (100% wool)
200g in brown (colour code 2), 80g in light brown (colour code 4)

5.5mm (US 9, UK 5) needles
Tapestry needle
Sewing needle
Sewing thread
Four buttons (small wood duffle toggles)
Wool carder or a wire brush of the type used to brush dogs and cats

TENSION (GAUGE)
14 stitches and 21 rows in a 10cm (4in) square

TECHNIQUES USED
p2tog (page 86), ssp (page 87), m1 (page 89), selvedges (page 83) and seams (page 91)

NOTE
As this pillow is sewn along the right sides, it is essential that the selvedges are regular.

INSTRUCTIONS
The whole piece is knitted in purl, apart from the last 8 rows.
Using brown yarn, cast on 52 sts.
Rows 1–39: purl.
Rows 40 and 41: *using light brown wool, purl.
Rows 42 and 43: using brown wool, purl.*
Repeat from * to * three more times (16 rows in total).
Next 16 rows: using light brown wool, purl.
Next 2 rows: *using brown wool, purl.
Next 2 rows: using light brown wool, purl.*
Repeat from * to * three more times (16 rows in total).
Next 70 rows: using brown wool, purl (ending in one knit row).
The piece is finished with a strip in purl, with buttonholes for the toggles.

Next 4 rows: purl.

First row for the buttonholes:
sl1p, k5, *ssp, p2tog, p8*, repeat from * to * until end of row, ssp, p2tog, p5, k1.

Second row for the buttonholes:
sl1p, p6, *m2, p10*, repeat from * to * until 7 sts before end of row, m2, p6, k1.
Next 4 rows: purl.
Cast off all sts.

FINISHING

Weave in the yarn ends, working them through the stitches on the reverse side.

Hand wash in warm water and a wool detergent, rubbing the knit together lightly to gently felt it.

Gently squeeze out any excess water and leave to dry flat.

Right side out, fold the piece into three, so that the striped section is centred at the front of the pillow and the area where the buttons are to be sewn, at the top of the piece, is under the strip with the respective buttonholes.

Using the yarn, sew the pillow seams along the side selvedges, right sides out.

With a wool carder, or a wire brush for pets, brush the surface of the pillow cover to create a soft, fluffy surface. Then sew on the toggles.

Poveira Leggings

The patterns on these leggings come from the Póvoa de Varzim fishermen's socks shown on page 45. They are a circular knit, worked with the reverse side facing, and use a soft yarn mix of wool and angora.

●●●○○

MATERIALS AND TOOLS
Yarn – Debbie Bliss Donegal Luxury Tweed Aran (85% wool, 15% angora):
90g in colour 26 (forest), 15g in colour 28 (yellow), 15g in colour 30 (pink), 20g in colour 10 (silver); alternatively, you could use The Fibre Co. Lore yarn or Retrosaria Beiroa yarn.

3.5mm (US 4, UK 9/10) double-pointed needles
4mm (US 6, UK 8) double-pointed needles
Stitch marker
Tapestry needle

TENSION (GAUGE)
20 stitches and 26 rows in a 10cm (4in) square

TECHNIQUES USED
Jacquard knitting (page 84)

PATTERN: USE CHART D (PAGE 148)

INSTRUCTIONS (MAKE TWO)
Using 3.5mm (US 4, UK 9/10) needles and colour 26, cast on 72 sts evenly between the four needles. Place a marker on the needle to mark the end/start of the round.
Rounds 1–12: work in rib stitch 2/2 (*p2, k2*, repeat from * to * until end of round).
Rounds 13–18: using 4mm (US 6, UK 8) needles, work in purl. Follow Chart D, continuing to purl with the 4mm (US 6, UK 8) needles. The ends of the coloured yarn that are being introduced should remain loose and will be woven in at the end.

Next 6 rounds: using colour 26, purl.
Next 12 rounds: using 3.5mm (US 4, UK 9/10) needles, work in rib stitch 2/2 (*p2, k2*, repeat from * to * until end of round). Cast off purl sts in purl, and knit sts in knit.

FINISHING
Weave the yarn ends through the stitches on the reverse side.

Striped Socks

These simple woollen socks follow the same basic pattern used for the majority of Portuguese handmade socks. The sock is knitted in the round in a continuous process from the top to the toe, with the heel shaped in four successive stages. The red and white stripes were inspired by the socks on page 40.

The method for making these socks has the following steps:
Cuff: the top of the sock, decorated with a picot edging or a few centimetres of rib stitch.
Leg: the tube, worked in purl using five needles, without any increases or decreases.
Back of the heel: a knitted square worked using only two needles.
Base of the heel: a knitted triangle worked using only two needles.
Instep: the side part of the foot under the ankles is worked in purl on five needles and shaped using symmetrical decreases.
Foot: always in purl, as for the leg.
Toe: narrowing to the end of the sock, worked in purl in the round, with simple p2tog decreases.

Completing your first pair of socks is a challenge worth taking on. Once the method for the various stages for the heel – which at first sight seems complex and confusing – has been understood, many people find that socks become one of the most enjoyable things to knit. This is made more attractive by the wide variety of yarns available that have been specifically designed for the purpose of sock-making.

SIZE
4–5 UK/ 37–38 European/ 6–7 US

MATERIALS AND TOOLS
50g Retrosaria Mé-Mé 2 Ply (100% wool) colour 1684
or Kauni 8/2 (100% wool) colour MM
50g Retrosaria Mé-Mé 2 Ply (100% wool) white
or Kauni 8/2 (100% wool) colour AA

Five 2.5mm (US 1.5, UK 12/13) double-pointed needles
Three markers
Narrow sewing needle for knits

TENSION (GAUGE)
14 stitches and 24 rows in a 5cm (2in) square

TECHNIQUES USED
Knitting with five needles (page 82), picot edging (page 93) or rib stitch (page 81), purling two together (page 86), slip slip purl (page 87), yarn over (page 88) and picking up (page 92)

INSTRUCTIONS

Using white wool, cast on 60 sts evenly between four needles (15 sts on each needle). Place a marker on the needle to mark the end/start of the round.

Make the picot edging in accordance with the instructions on page 93 or, alternatively, work the band in rib stitch: work 20 rounds in rib stitch 2/2 (*p2, k2*, repeat from * to * until end of round).

Sock leg:

Striped pattern (*the threads should not be cut at the end of each stripe but passed through to the reverse of the piece*):

Next 5 rounds: *using red yarn, purl.

Next 5 rounds: using white yarn, purl.*

Next rounds: follow the pattern from * to * six times.

Next 5 rounds: using red yarn, purl. Cut red yarn, leaving around 10cm (4in) to be woven in at the end.

Next 2 rounds: using white yarn, purl.

Back of the heel:

The back of the heel is worked in a flat knit using white yarn for half of the sts and alternating a row of purl and knit. The remaining sts should be left until they are needed.

Next round: p15, turn piece around.

Next round: *take the free needle in your right hand, sl1k, k29, turn piece around.

Next round: sl1p, p29, turn piece around.*

Next rounds: repeat from * to * until back of heel has 30 rows, and finish with a purl row.

Turn piece around.

Base of the heel:

The base of the heel is the continuation of the back of the heel. It is shaped through a combination of short rows and symmetrical decreases, as follows:

Row 1: sl1k, k16, k2tog, k1, turn piece around.
Row 2: sl1p, p5, p2tog, p1, turn piece around.
Row 3: sl1k, k6, k2tog, k1, turn piece around.
Row 4: sl1p, p7, p2tog, p1, turn piece around.
Row 5: sl1k, k8, k2tog, k1, turn piece around.
Row 6: sl1p, p9, p2tog, p1, turn piece around.
Row 7: sl1k, k10, k2tog, k1, turn piece around.
Row 8: sl1p, p11, p2tog, p1, turn piece around.
Row 9: sl1k, k12, k2tog, k1, turn piece around.

Row 10: sl1p, p13, p2tog, p1, turn piece around.
Row 11: sl1k, k14, k2tog, k1, turn piece around.
Row 12: sl1p, p15, p2tog, p1 (18 sts).

Edges: The process

At this stage, 15 sts are picked up from each selvedge from the back of the heel and the work continues as a circular knit using all five needles, gradually decreasing the perimeter of the sock until it is back to the initial 60 sts. The rest of the sock is worked in purl.

Side increases:

Pick up 15 sts on to the left selvedge from the back of the heel. Place a marker on the right-hand needle (this is marker A). Work the 30 sts from the instep (those not being used). Place a marker on the right-hand needle (this is marker B).

Pick up 15 sts on the other selvedge from the back of the heel. Work until end of round, as indicated by the start/end marker that was placed at the start of the piece (78 sts).

Decreases:

The decreases are made symmetrically, always at the same point – before marker A and after marker B – in alternate rows.

Next round: *work up to 2 sts before marker A, 1ssp (then move the marker to the needle in the right hand), work up to marker B (and move the marker to the needle in the right hand), p2tog, work to end of round.

Next round: purl.*

The pattern of stripes starts again at this point, beginning with a red stripe:

Starting with red yarn (and changing the colour in accordance with the pattern), repeat from * to * until there are only 60 sts left on needles, work to end of round.

Markers A and B can now be removed.

Continuing to follow the stripe pattern, work 50 rounds, finishing with a red round.

Cut the red yarn, leaving approximately 10cm (4in).

Toe: The process

The next phase is to narrow the toe using simple purling two together decreases, which are made on the last sts of each needle. Before working the toe, it is advisable to try the sock on and check that it covers the base of the toes. For a longer foot, work some extra rounds with the white yarn before starting the decreases.

Count the number of sts on each needle: there should be 15. If necessary, redistribute the sts over the four needles so they are equal (60 sts in total).

Next round: using white yarn, *work all sts from the needle in the left hand apart from the last two. Work the last 2 sts from the left-hand needle together and slip the resulting stitch onto the empty needle, which is now the new right-hand needle.*
The start/end marker can now be removed.
Repeat from * to * until there are only 2 sts left on each needle. Cut the yarn leaving a length of approximately 20cm (7¾in), and with the tapestry needle, pass the yarn through the remaining 8 sts, pulling them tight to close the piece.

FINISHING

Weave all loose ends through the stitches on the reverse side. Repeat the instructions from the beginning to complete the pair.

Woolly Hat

Woollen bowl [*Tigela de lã*] is the name given to the loose caps formerly used by men in the region of Castro Daire. They are made from a fine handspun wool, and fit the head loosely so they can be worn comfortably under other headwear. These caps are still made by the women of the Montemuro Ethnographic Association, and are usually made from white wool with dark brown patterns.

●●●○○

MATERIALS AND TOOLS
30g Retrosaria Mé-Mé 22 (100% wool) in pale brown
or Kauni 8/2 (100% wool) colour PP1
10g Retrosaria Mé-Mé 22 (100% wool) in white
or Kauni 8/2 (100% wool) colour AA

Five 2mm (US 0, UK 14) double-pointed needles
Small stitch marker
Tapestry needle

TENSION (GAUGE)
18 stitches and 27 rows in a 5cm (2in) square

TECHNIQUES USED
Single casting on (page 75), five needle knitting (page 82), pointed edging (page 93), purling two together (page 86) and yarn over (page 88)

INSTRUCTIONS
Using brown wool, cast on 148 sts evenly between the four needles using the single casting-on method. Place a marker on the needle to mark the end/start of the round and work the picot edging following the instructions on page 93.

Rounds 1 and 2: purl.

Round 3: *yo, p2tog*, repeat from * to * until end of round (148 sts).

Rounds 4 and 5: purl.

Round 6: *yo, p2tog*, repeat from * to * until end of round (148 sts).

Rounds 7 and 8: purl.

Round 9: knit.

From this point on, the rest of the piece is worked in purl.

Striped pattern (*the threads should not be cut at the end of each stripe and should instead be passed through to the reverse of the piece*):

Rounds 10–16: *using brown yarn, purl.

Rounds 17 and 18: using white yarn, purl.*

Next rounds: follow the pattern from * to * five times (45 rounds).

Next 7 rounds: using brown yarn, purl.

Count the number of sts on each needle: there should be 37. If necessary, redistribute the sts over the four needles so they are equal. Remove the marker.

The next phase is to narrow the cap using p2tog decreases, which are made on the last sts of each needle as follows:

Using white yarn, *work all the sts on the needle in the left hand apart from the last 2. Purl the last 2 sts from the left-hand needle together (p2tog) and pass the resulting stitch onto the empty needle, which is now the new right-hand needle.* Following the pattern (7 brown rounds, 2 white rounds), repeat from * to * until there are only 2 sts left on each needle. Cut the yarn leaving a length of approximately 20cm (8in), and with the tapestry needle, pass the yarn through the remaining 8 sts, pulling them tight to close the top.

FINISHING
Weave in the yarn ends, working them through the stitches
on the reverse side.

Caninhas Shawl

The delicate stitches of this shawl are traditionally made in some regions using a pair of thin hooked needles and a section of smooth bamboo cane with a bevelled tip (see page 65), hence the name, meaning 'shawl of the canines'. Here a 12mm (US 0, UK 14) needle is substituted for the original bamboo cane.

All the stitches are worked in purl (including the first of each row). The lacy pattern is achieved by crossing groups of 6 stitches, which can be done in two different ways. The pattern is completed every 8 rows.

● ● ● ● ○

MATERIALS AND TOOLS

270g Atelier Zitron Filigran (100% wool) colour 2515

2mm (US 0, UK 14) circular needles
12mm (US 17, UK 000) circular needles
Cable needle
Tapestry needle

TENSION (GAUGE)

34 stitches and 36 rows in a 10cm (4in) square

TECHNIQUES USED

Crossed stitches (see below)

INSTRUCTIONS

Cast on 172 sts onto the 2mm (US 0, UK 14) needles.

Row 1–6: purl.

Cane row: work a row using the 12mm (US 17, UK 000) needle.

Cross row: choose one of the following methods and use it for the rest of the shawl.

For the first method the sts cross on the reverse side, and for the second, less common method, the sts cross in between each other.

Method 1 (with the cable needle):

Using the 2mm (US 0, UK 14) needle, work 2 sts, *place the following 3 sts on the cable needle (which hangs behind the piece). Work 3 sts from the needle in the left hand and then the 3 sts from the auxiliary needle, being careful not to twist them.* Repeat from * to * until there are just 2 sts remaining on the left-hand needle. Work these 2 sts as normal.

Method 2 (with the hooked needle):

Using the 2mm (US 0, UK 14) needle, work 2 sts. *With the aid of the hook, slip the 4th, 5th and 6th sts from the left-hand needle over the first 3 sts and work them using the 2mm needle in order (4th, 5th, 6th, 1st, 2nd, 3rd)*. Repeat from * to

* until there are just 2 sts remaining on the left-hand needle. Work these 2 sts as normal.

Work 6 rows using the 2mm needles. Repeat the cane row, and then the cross rows, repeat from * to * until the shawl is approximately 2m (2¼yd) long. Purl 6 rows.

Cast off.

FINISHING

Weave in the yarn ends, working them under the stitches. Carefully wash the shawl in lukewarm water with mild wool soap. Using a towel, gently squeeze out the excess water without twisting the shawl. Lay out the damp shawl over a towel on a bed or carpet. Stretch it gently so that it regains its rectangular shape. Fasten with pins, and leave it to dry in this position.

Corvo Island Beret

This traditional woollen beret from Corvo Island (see page 50) is reproduced here using a lovely llama hair yarn, which gives a softer appearance than the sheep's wool it would have originally been made from.

●●●○○

MATERIALS AND TOOLS

100g Mirasol Miski (100% llama) colour 11 (grey) or 13 (orange)
20g Mirasol Miski (100% llama) colour 3 (white)

4mm (US 6, UK 8) 40cm (15¾in) long circular needles (optional)
4mm (US 6, UK 8) double-pointed needles
Tapestry needle
Sheet of graph paper
Pencil

TECHNIQUES USED

Knitting with five needles (page 82), jacquard (page 84), picot edgings (page 93) and purling two together (page 86)

TENSION (GAUGE)

12 stitches and 13 rows in a 5cm (2in) square

PREPARATION

Design the desired name or text to work into the reverse side of the edge of the beret on the graph paper. The letters should be a maximum of six squares. Invert the text vertically so that the letters are oriented in the same way as the example shown in Chart E.

PATTERN: USE CHARTS E & F (PAGE 148)

INSTRUCTIONS

Using the grey yarn, cast on 120 sts using the single casting-on method as shown on page 75, distributed equally over the four needles (30 sts on each needle), or along the circular needles, and place a marker to show the end/start of the round.

Round 1: purl.

Rounds 2–7: purl, working in the chosen text (Chart E) with white yarn in jacquard. The white yarn should be cut at each round whenever it is no longer needed, leaving about a 10cm (4in) length to weave in later.

Round 8: using grey wool, purl.

Round 9: knit.

Rounds 10–17: purl.

Using the tapestry needle, weave in the yarn ends, working them through the sts on the reverse side.

For the following round, the cast-on sts are worked together with those from the needle, as explained on page 93 (pointed edging).

Next round: purl.

Next rounds: introduce the white yarn and follow the pattern in Chart F in jacquard (11 rounds) in purl.

Cut the white yarn, leaving approximately 10cm (4in).

Next round: using grey yarn, *p6, m1*, repeat from * to * until end of round (140 sts).

Next 2 rounds: purl.

Next round: *p7, m1*, repeat from * to * until end of round (160 sts).

Next 10 rounds: purl.

Next round: *p8, p2tog*, repeat from * to * until end of round (144 sts).

Next 3 rounds: purl.

Next round: p3, p2tog, *p7, p2tog*, repeat from * to * until 4 sts before end of round, p4 (128 sts).

Next 3 rounds: purl.

Next round: *p6, p2tog*, repeat from * to * until end of round (112 sts).

Next 3 rounds: purl.

Next round: p2, p2tog, *p5, p2tog*, repeat from * to * until 3 sts before end of round, p3 (96 sts).

Next 2 rounds: purl.

When working with circular needles, from this point on it is necessary to move the piece to the double-pointed needles, as the perimeter of the beret will be too short.

Next round: *p4, p2tog*, repeat from * to * until end of round (80 sts).

Next 2 rounds: purl.

Next round: p1, p2tog, *p3, p2tog*, repeat from * to * until 2 sts before end of round, p2 (64 sts).

Next 2 rounds: purl.

Next round: *p2, p2tog*, repeat from * to * until end of round (48 sts).

Next 2 rounds: purl.

Next round: *p2tog, p1*, repeat from * to * until end of round (32 sts).

Next 2 rounds: purl.

Next round: *p2tog*, repeat from * to * until end of round (16 sts).

Cut the yarn leaving a length of approximately 20cm (7¾in) and, using the tapestry needle, pass the yarn through the 16 remaining sts, pulling them tight to close the piece.

FINISHING

Weave in the yarn ends, working them through the stitches on the reverse side. Make a pompom and sew it to the top of the beret.

Concha Socks

Concha socks [*meias de concha*], which are still made in certain regions of northeast Portugal (see page 42), are an excellent example of the use of slipped stitches to produce two-coloured patterns without passing the yarn through the reverse, as is so characteristic of jacquard. The pattern shown here was inspired by a pair purchased in Trás-os-Montes in the 1980s. The socks are worked from the wrong side in purl.

●●●●○

SIZE
4–5 UK/ 37–38 European/ 6–7 US

MATERIALS AND TOOLS
50g Retrosaria Bucos Meia (100% wool) in brown
50g Retrosaria Bucos Meia (100% wool) in white

2mm (US 0, UK 14) double-pointed needles
2.5mm (US 1.5, UK 12/13) double-pointed needles
Three stitch markers
Tapestry needle

TENSION (GAUGE)
16 stitches and 28 rows in a 5cm (2in) square

TECHNIQUES USED
Knitting with five needles (page 82), picot edging (page 93) or rib stitch (page 81), slip stitches (page 85), purling two together (page 86), slip slip purl (page 87), make one increase (page 89), yarn over (page 88) and picking up (page 92)

INSTRUCTIONS

Using the white wool and the 2mm (US 0, UK 14) needles, cast on 60 sts evenly between the four needles (15 sts on each needle). Place a marker on the needle to mark the end/start of the round.

Make the picot edging following the instructions on page 93 or, alternatively, make the top of the socks in rib stitch: work 20 rounds in rib stitch 2/2 (*p2, k2*, repeat from * to * until end of round).

Sock leg:
Next 6 rounds: using 2.5mm (US 1.5, UK 12/13) needles, purl.
Next 2 rounds: using brown yarn (leave white yarn uncut), purl.

The threads should not be cut at the end of each stripe and should instead be passed through the reverse side.
Next 2 rounds: using white wool, purl.
The pattern using the slipped stitch technique starts at this point, after which 2 rounds with brown wool and 2 rounds with white wool are alternated.
All of the leg part of the sock is worked in purl.

Shell pattern (complete after 20 rounds):
Rounds 1 and 2: using brown yarn, *work 4 sts, sl1p*, repeat from * to *.
Rounds 3 and 4: using white yarn, p3, *sl1p, p4*, repeat from * to * until 2 sts before end of second round, sl1p, p1.

Rounds 5 and 6: using brown yarn, p2, *sl1p, p4*, repeat from * to * until 3 sts before end of second round, sl1p, p2.

Rounds 7 and 8: using white yarn, work p1, *sl1p, p4*, repeat from * to * until 4 sts before end of second round, sl1p, p3.

Rounds 9 and 10: using brown yarn, work *sl1p, p4*, repeat from * to * until the end of two rounds.

Rounds 11 and 12: using white yarn, *p4, sl1p*, repeat from * to * until the end of two rounds.

Rounds 13 and 14: using brown yarn, p3 *sl1p, p4*, repeat from * to * until 2 sts before the end of the second round. sl1p, p1.

Rounds 15 and 16: using white yarn, p2, *sl1p, p4*, repeat from * to * until 3 sts before the end of the second round, sl1p, p2.

Rounds 17 and 18: using brown yarn, work p1, *sl1p, p4*, repeat from * to * until 4 sts before the end of the second round, sl1p, p3.

Rounds 19 and 20: using white yarn, work *sl1p, p4*, repeat from * to * until the end of 2 rounds.

Work through the pattern three times (in total).

Using brown yarn, *p4, sl1p*, repeat from * to * until the end of the second round.

Next 2 rounds: using white yarn, work p3, *sl1p, p4*, repeat from * to * until 2 sts before the end of the second round, sl1p, p1.

Cut the yarn, leaving around 10cm (4in) to be woven in at the end.

Using brown yarn, p2 *sl1p, p4*, repeat from * to * until 3 sts before end of round. sl1p, p2.

Back of the heel:
The back of the heel is worked in a flat knit using just 30 sts. For the knit rows, the sts that are slipped are always then taken up in purl, keeping the yarn on the reverse side of the piece.

Row 1: turn piece around, k2, sl1p, k4, sl1p, k4, sl1p, k4, sl1p, k4, sl1p, k4, sl1p, k2 (30 sts).

Row 2: turn piece around, using white yarn, m1, p1, *sl1p, p4*, repeat from * to * until 4 sts before end of row. sl1p, p3, m1 (32 sts).

Row 3: turn piece around, sl1k, k3, *sl1p, k4*, repeat from * to * until 3 sts before end of row. sl1p, k2.

Row 4: turn piece around, using brown yarn, sl2p, p4. *sl1p, p1*, repeat from * to * until 4 sts before end of row, p1.

Row 5: turn piece around, sl1k, k4, *sl1p, k4*, repeat from * to * until 3 sts before end of row, sl1p, k1.

Row 6: turn piece around, using white yarn, work *sl1p, p4*, repeat from * to * until 2 sts before end of row, sl1p, p1.

Row 7: turn piece around, sl1k, *sl1p, k4*, repeat from * to * until 1 st before end of row. k1.

Row 8: turn piece around, using brown yarn, sl1p, p3, *sl1p, p4*, repeat from * to * until 3 sts before end of row, sl1p, p2.

Row 9: turn piece around, sl1k, k1, *sl1p, k4*, repeat from * to * until end of row.

Row 10: turn piece around, using white yarn, sl1p, p2, *sl1p, p4*, repeat from * to * until 4 sts before end of row, sl1p, p3.

Row 11: turn piece around, sl1k, k2, *sl1p, k4*, repeat from * to * until 4 sts before end of row, sl1p, k3.

Row 12: turn piece around, using brown yarn, sl1p, p1, *sl1p, p4*, repeat from * to * until end of row.

Row 13: turn piece around, sl1k, k3, *sl1p, k4*, repeat from * to * until 3 sts before end of row, sl1p, k2.

Row 14: turn piece around, using white yarn, work *sl2p, p4*, *sl1p, p4*, repeat from * to * until 1 st before end of row, p1.

Row 15: turn piece around, sl1k, k4, *sl1p, k4*, repeat from * to * until 2 sts before end of row, sl1p, k1.

Row 16: turn piece around, using brown yarn, *sl1p, p4*, repeat from * to * until 2 sts before end of row, sl1p, p1.

Row 17: turn piece around, sl1k, *sl1p, k4*, repeat from * to * until 1 st before end of round, k1.

Row 18: turn piece around, using white yarn sl1p, p3, *sl1p, p4*, repeat from * to * until 3 sts before end of row, sl1p, p2.

Row 19: turn piece around, sl1k, k1, *sl1p, k4*, repeat from * to * until end of row.

Row 20: turn piece around; using brown yarn sl1p, p2, *sl1p, p4*, repeat from * to * until 4 sts before end of row, sl1p, p3.

Row 21: turn piece around, sl1k, k2, *sl1p, k4*, repeat from * to * until 4 sts before end of row, sl1p, k3.

Row 22: turn piece around, using white yarn sl1p, p1, *sl1p, p4*, repeat from * to * until end of row.

Row 23: turn piece around, sl1k, k3 *sl1p, k4*, repeat from * to * until 3 sts before end of row, sl1p, k2.

Row 24: turn piece around, using brown yarn, *sl2p, p4*, *sl1p, p4*, repeat from * to * until 1 st before end of row, p1.

Row 25: turn piece around, sl1k, k4, *sl1p, k4*, repeat from * to * until 2 sts before end of row, sl1p, k1.

Row 26: turn piece around, using white yarn, work *sl1p, p4*, repeat from * to * until 1 st before end of row, sl1p, p1.

Row 27: turn piece around, sl1k, *sl1p, k4*, repeat from * to * until 1 st before end of round, k1.

Row 28: turn piece around, using brown yarn, *sl1p, p3*, *sl1p, p4*, repeat from * to * until 3 sts before end of row, sl1p, p2.

Row 29: turn piece around, sl1k, k1, *sl1p, k4*, repeat from * to * until end of row.

Cut the brown yarn, leaving around 10cm (4in) to be cast off at the end.

Row 30: turn piece around, using white yarn, sl1p and work all sts in purl up to end of row.

Base of the heel (using white yarn):

Row 1: sl1k, k16, k2tog, k1 (19 sts on right-hand needle), turn piece around.
Row 2: sl1p, p3, p2tog, p1, turn piece around.
Row 3: sl1k, k4, k2tog, k1, turn piece around.
Row 4: sl1p, p5, p2tog, p1, turn piece around.
Row 5: sl1k, k6. k2tog, k1, turn piece around.
Row 6: sl1p, p7, p2tog, p1, turn piece around.
Row 7: sl1k, k8. k2tog. k1, turn piece around.
Row 8: sl1p, p9, p2tog, p1, turn piece around.
Row 9: sl1k, k10. k2tog. k1, turn piece around.
Row 10: sl1p, p11, p2tog, p1, turn piece around.
Row 11: sl1k, k12, k2tog. k1, turn piece around.
Row 12: sl1p, p13, p2tog, p1, turn piece around.
Row 13: sl1k, 1k4. k2tog. k1, turn piece around.
Row 14: sl1p, p15, p2tog, p1 (18 sts).

Edges:

Side increases:

Using brown yarn, pick up 15 sts on the left selvedge from the back of the heel. Place a marker on the right-hand needle (this marker is marker A).

Work the 30 sts from the instep (those that were not being used) as follows: p2, *sl1p, p4*, repeat from * to * up to the 15th st (inclusive). sl1p, k2. Place a marker on the right-hand needle (this marker is marker B).

Pick up 15 sts on the other selvedge from the back of the heel. Work the 18 sts from the base of the heel as follows: p1, *sl1p, p4*, repeat from * to * up to the 16th st (inclusive), sl1p, p1.

Decreases:

Following the pattern, the decreases are made symmetrically, always at the same point (before marker A and after marker B) – on alternate rows.

Round 1: using white yarn, p2, *sl1p, p4*, repeat from * to * up to 3 sts before marker A, sl1p, ssp, p1, *sl1p, p4*, repeat from * to * until 4 sts before marker B, sl1p, p3, p2tog, p3, *sl1p, p4*, repeat from * to * until 3 sts before end of round, sl1p, p2.

Round 2: p2, *sl1p, p4*, repeat from * to * until 2 sts before marker A, sl1p, p1, p1, *sl1p, p4*, repeat from * to * until 4 sts before marker B, sl1p, p3, p4, *sl1p, p4*, repeat from * to * until 3 sts before end of round, sl1p, p2.

Round 3: using brown yarn, p1, *sl1p, p4*, repeat from * to * until 3 sts before marker A, sl1p, ssp, *sl1p, p4*, repeat from * to * up to marker B, p2tog, p1, *sl1p, p4*, repeat from * to * until 4 sts before end of round, sl1p, p3.

Round 4: p1 *sl1p, p4*, repeat from * to * until 2 sts before marker A, sl1p, p1, *sl1p, p4*, repeat from * to * until marker B, p2, *sl1p, p4*, repeat from * to * until 4 sts before end of round, sl1p, p3.

Round 5: using white yarn, *sl1p, p4*, repeat from * to * up to 3 sts before marker A, sl1p, ssp, p4, *sl1p, p4*, repeat from * to * until 1 st before marker B, sl1p, p2tog, p4, *sl1p, p4*, repeat from * to * until end of round.

Round 6: *sl1p, p4*, repeat from * to * until 2 sts before marker A, sl1p, p1, p4, *sl1p, p4*, repeat from * to * up to 1 st before marker B, sl1p, slp5, *sl1p, p4*, repeat from * to * until end of round.

Round 7: using brown yarn, p4, *sl1p, p4*, repeat from * to * until 3 sts before marker A, sl1p, ssp, p3, *sl1p, p4*, repeat from * to * until 2 sts before marker B, sl1p, p1, p2tog, p2, *sl1p, p4*, repeat from * to * until 1 st before end of round, sl1p.

Round 8: p4, *sl1p, p4*, repeat from * to * until 2 sts before marker A, sl1p, p1, p3, *sl1p, p4*, repeat from * to * until 2 sts before marker B, sl1p, p1, p3, *sl1p, p4*, repeat from * to * until 1 st before end of round, sl1p.

Round 9: using white yarn, p3, *sl1p, p4*, repeat from * to * until 3 sts before marker A, sl1p, ssp, p2, *sl1p, p4*, repeat from * to * until 3 sts before marker B, sl1p, p2, p2tog, *sl1p, p4*, repeat from * to * until 2 sts before end of round, sl1p, p1.

Round 10: p3, *sl1p, p4*, repeat from * to * until 2 sts before marker A, sl1p, p1, p2, *sl1p, p4*, repeat from * to * until 3 sts before marker B, sl1p, p2, p1, *sl1p, p4*, repeat from * to * until 2 sts before end of round, sl1p, p1.

Round 11: using brown yarn, p2, sl1p, p4, sl1p, ssp, p1, *sl1p, p4*, repeat from * to * until 4 sts before marker B, sl1p, p3. p2tog, p3, *sl1p, p4*, repeat from * to * until 3 sts before end of round, sl1p, p2.

Round 12: p2, sl1p, p4, sl1p, p1, p1, *sl1p, p4*, repeat from * to * until 4 sts before marker B, sl1p, p3, p4, *sl1p, p4*, repeat from * to * until 3 sts before end of round, sl1p, p2.

Round 13: using white yarn, p1, sl1p, p4, sl1p, ssp, *sl1p, p4*, repeat from * to * up to marker B, p2tog, p1, *sl1p, p4*, repeat from * to * until 4 sts before end of round, sl1p, p3.

Round 14: p1, sl1p, p4, sl1p, p1, *sl1p, p4*, repeat from * to * up to marker B, p2, *sl1p, p4*, repeat from * to * until 4 sts before end of round, sl1p, p3.

Round 15: using brown yarn, sl1p, p4, sl1p, ssp, p4, *sl1p, p4*, repeat from * to * until 1 st before marker B, sl1p, p2tog, p4, *sl1p, p4*, repeat from * to * until end of round.

Round 16: sl1p, p4, sl1p, p1, p4, *sl1p, p4*, repeat from * to * until 1 st before marker B, sl1p, p5, *sl1p, p4*, repeat from * to * until end of round.

Round 17: using white yarn, p4, sl1p, ssp, p3, *sl1p, p4*, repeat from * to * until 2 sts before marker B, sl1p, p1, p2tog, p2, *sl1p, p4*, repeat from * to * until 1 st before end of round, sl1p (60 sts).

Markers A and B can be removed from the needles at this point.

Following round: *p4, sl1p*, repeat from * to * until 1 st before end of round, sl1p.

Repeat the pattern for 64 rounds, starting at round 13.

Toe:

Before working the toe, it is advisable to try the sock on and check that it covers the underside of the toes. For larger feet, work some extra rounds of the shell pattern, ending with two rounds of the white yarn.

Next 2 rounds: using brown yarn, purl. Cut the brown yarn, leaving approximately 10cm (4in).

Count the number of sts on each needle: there should be 15. If necessary, redistribute the sts over the four needles so they are equal (60 sts in total).

Using white yarn, *work all the sts on the needle in the left hand apart from the last two. Work the last 2 sts from the left-hand needle together and slip the resulting st onto the empty needle, which is now the new right-hand needle.*

The start/end marker can now be removed.

Repeat from * to * until there are only 2 sts left on each needle. Cut the yarn leaving a length of approximately 20cm (7¾in), and use the tapestry needle to pass the yarn through the 8 remaining sts, pulling them tight to close the piece.

FINISHING

Weave in the yarn ends, working them through the stitches on the reverse side.

Repeat instructions from the beginning, to complete the pair.

Gloves

These fingerless gloves were inspired by a pair in the collection of the National Museum of Ancient Art (image 42, page 60). These are made from a very fine, soft wool, and are embroidered in cross stitch once completed. The piece is circular and is worked using five needles, almost all in purl. The thumbhole is created through simple symmetrical increases from the base of the hand. The top of the glove has two separate steps: first the thumb and then the holes for the other fingers.

MATERIALS AND TOOLS
25g Brooklyn Tweed Loft (100% wool) colour Long Johns
To embroider: Aurifil lana (50% wool, 50% acrylic) in 8212, 8515 and 8328

2.5mm (US 1.5, UK 12/13) double-pointed needles
3 small markers
Safety pins to secure stitches or extra 2.5mm needles
Tapestry needle

TENSION (GAUGE)
15 stitches and 23 rows in a 5 x 5cm (2in) square

TECHNIQUES USED
Knitting with five needles (page 82), make one increase (page 89), pointed edging (page 93) and casting off in knit (page 90)

EMBROIDERY: USE CHART G (PAGE 148)

INSTRUCTIONS
Cast on (page 75) 48 sts singly, evenly distributed between the four needles. Place a marker on the needle to mark the end/start of the round and make the pointed edging following the instructions on page 93.
Repeat the pattern twice from the base of the fist:
Pattern for the base of the fist:
Round 1: knit.
Round 2: purl.
Round 3: *k3, p1*, repeat from * to * until end of round.
Round 4: purl.
Round 5: p1, k1, *p3, k1*, repeat from * to * until end of round.
Rounds 6 and 7: purl.
Repeat these 7 rows.
Fist and hand (in purl):
Note: the marker for the start/end of the round is not mentioned in the following instructions. The markers referred

to are those that indicate the position of the increases from the base of the thumb.
Next 15 rounds: purl.
Next round: p1, m1. Place a marker on the right-hand needle (marker A) and work up until last st of round. Place another marker on right-hand needle (marker B), m1, p1 (50 sts).
Next round: *work up until marker A, m1. Pass the marker on to the right-hand needle and work up to marker B. Pass marker onto right-hand needle, m1. Work to end of round* (52 sts).
Following rounds: repeat from * to * until you have made a total of 16 increased sts (64 sts).
Next 20 rounds: without removing the markers, purl.
Thumb (in purl):
The thumb is worked circularly in 16 of the 18 sts between the markers that indicate the location of the increases plus an

additional 2 sts for the connection between the thumb and the hand. From this point the five needles will be used only to work the thumb section, so the remaining sts should be placed on stitch holders or on spare needles.

Work up to 1 st before marker A. Cast on 2 sts on the right-hand needle and join the circle corresponding to the thumb, working the first st after marker B. Work until end of round (18 sts).

Next 10 rounds: purl.

Cast off the 18 sts for the thumb in knit.

Fingers:

Redistribute the sts over the 4 needles, removing the markers (48 sts).

The piece starts anew with the connection between the hand and the thumb, picking up 2 new sts from the base of the two additional sts cast on for the thumb (50 sts in total). This needs to be done with care, so that the new sts do not appear too open.

The marker for the end/start of the round is placed between the 2 new sts.

Next 14 rounds: purl.

Next round: *knit.

Next round: purl.*

Repeat from * to * twice (6 rounds in total).

Cast off in knit.

FINISHING

Weave in the yarn ends, working them through the stitches on the reverse side.

Repeat for the second glove and embroider the designs.

Lace Collar

The lace used on this cotton blouse is one of many examples of Portuguese lace made with two needles to decorate sheets, underwear and other pieces. The principle is the same as for the scarf on page 104, but in this case the stitch is more complex, and demands concentration as it uses fine thread and very thin needles. As is usual for *rendas por música* ['lace by music'], purl stitch is used. The notation for this kind of work differs in that it uses a simple code (hence the 'music'), where O means a yarn over increase, X a purl two together decrease and numbers (the number of purl stitches). Therefore, the first lines of the pattern are notated as follows:

4OX9XO1OX
O1O3OX8OX4
4OX7XO5OX

●●●●●

MATERIALS AND TOOLS (for approximately 1m/1yd of lace)
50g Limol Mercer Especial no. 60 (100% cotton) in white

1.75mm (US 00, UK 17) needles
Tapestry needle

TENSION (GAUGE)
5 stitches and 10 rows in a 1cm (⅜in) square

TECHNIQUES USED
Purling two together (page 86) and yarn over (page 88)

NOTE
This lace uses double decreases, where 3 stitches are purled together.

INSTRUCTIONS
Row 1: cast on 20 sts.
Row 2: p4, yo, p2tog, p9, p2tog, yo, p1, yo, p2tog (20 sts).
Row 3: yo, p1, yo, p3, yo, p2tog, p8, yo, p2tog, p4 (22 sts).
Row 4: p4, yo, p2tog, p7, p2tog, yo, p5, yo, p2tog (22 sts).
Row 5: yo, p1, yo, p1, yo, p2tog, p1, p2tog, yo, p1, yo, p2tog, p6, yo, p2tog, p4 (24 sts).
Row 6: p4, yo, p2tog, p5, p2tog, yo, p3, yo, p3tog, yo, p3, yo, p2tog (24 sts).
Row 7: yo, p1, yo, p11, yo, p2tog, p4, yo, p2tog, p4 (26 sts).
Row 8: p4, yo, p2tog, p3, p2tog, yo, p1, yo, p2tog, p1, p2tog, yo, p1, yo, p2tog, p1, p2tog, yo, p1, yo, p2tog (26 sts).
Row 9: yo, p1, yo, p3, yo, p3tog, yo, p3, yo, p3tog, yo, p3, yo, p2tog, p2, yo, p2tog, p4 (28 sts).

Row 10: p4, yo, p2tog, p1, p2tog, yo, p17, yo, p2tog (28 sts).
Row 11: yo, p2tog, yo, p2tog, p1, p2tog, yo, p1, yo, p2tog, p1, p2tog, yo, p1, yo, p2tog, p1, p2tog, yo, p3, yo, p2tog, p4 (28 sts).
Row 12: p4, yo, p2tog, p4, yo, p3tog, yo, p3, yo, p3tog, yo, p3, yo, p3tog, yo, p3tog (26 sts).
Row 13: yo, p2tog, yo, p2tog, p11, yo, p5, yo, p2tog, p4 (27 sts).
Row 14: p4, yo, p2tog, p6, yo, p3tog, p1, p2tog, yo, p1, yo, p2tog, p1, p2tog, yo, p3tog (24 sts).
Row 15: yo, p2tog, yo, p3tog, yo, p3, yo, p3tog, yo, p7, yo, p2tog, p4 (24 sts).
Row 16: p4, yo, p2tog, p8, yo, p2tog, p3, p2tog, yo, p3tog (22 sts).
Row 17: yo, p2tog, yo, p2tog, p1, p2tog, yo, p9, yo, p2tog, p4 (22 sts).

Row 18: p4, yo, p2tog, p10, yo, p3tog, yo, p3tog (20 sts).
Row 19: yo, p3tog, yo, p11, yo, p2tog, p4 (20 sts).
Repeat as many times as necessary to achieve the desired length.
Cast off all sts in purl.

Algibeira Pouch

The design of this piece was inspired by a number of old Portuguese and Spanish pouches. It uses thin needles so the fabric has a firm structure.

●●●●○

MATERIALS AND TOOLS
25g Retrosaria Mé-Mé 2 Ply (100% wool) colour 1684 or Kauni 8/2 (100% wool) colour MM2
10g Retrosaria Mé-Mé 2 ply (100% wool) colour 1610 or Kauni 8/2 (100% wool) colour JJ3
5g Retrosaria Mé-Mé 2 ply (100% wool) colour 1692 or Kauni 8/2 (100% wool) colour JJ7
5g Retrosaria Mé-Mé 2 ply (100% wool) colour 1788 or Kauni 8/2 (100% wool) colour KK2

2mm (US 0, UK 14) double-pointed needles
Two stitch markers
Tapestry needle

TENSION (GAUGE)
18 stitches and 20 rows in a 5cm (2in) square

TECHNIQUES USED
Knitting with five needles (page 82), jacquard (page 84), purling two together (page 86), slip slip purl (page 87), and make one increase (page 89)

PATTERN: USE CHART H (page 149)

INSTRUCTIONS
Using red wool, cast on 78 sts evenly between the four needles. Place a marker on the needle to mark the end/start of the round.
Round 1: purl
Round 2: knit.
Round 3: purl.
Round 4: knit.
Next 3 rounds: purl.
Next round: p3, p2tog, yo, * p4, p2tog, yo*, repeat from * to * until 6 loops are created; p7, p2tog, yo, * p4, p2tog, yo*, repeat from * to * until 4 sts before end of round, p4.
Next 2 rounds: purl.
Follow Chart H in jacquard, using purl throughout.
Next 2 rounds: purl.

Next round: p39, place a marker (marker B), work in purl until end of round (marker A).
Next round: p2tog with pink, *p1 red, p1 pink*, repeat from * to * until 3 sts before marker B; p1 red, ssp pink, p2tog pink, *p1 red, p1 pink*, repeat from * to * until 3 sts before marker A, p1 red, ssp pink.
Next rounds: Repeat the previous round until there are 6 sts left on the needles.
Cut the yarn leaving a length of approximately 20cm (7¾), and use the sewing needle to pass the yarn through the remaining 6 sts, pulling them tight to close the piece.

FINISHING

Weave in the yarn ends, working them through the sts on the reverse side. Make three small tassels for the corners of the triangle at the base of the pouch. Make two cords of about 50cm (19¾in) from the yarn used for the rest of the piece and pass each one through its row of openings at the top of the pouch, with one coming out at the top right, and the other at the top left of the pouch. Finish each string with a tassel.

Serra de Ossa Leggings

The pattern that decorates this piece, which is usually worked in yellow on a red background, is one of the most common for traditional Serra de Ossa knitted socks (see page 47). These leggings use Shetland wool in light beige with stripes of six different colours. They are worked from the wrong side in purl, with a ribbed band at each end.

●●●●○

MATERIALS AND TOOLS
Jamieson & Smith 2-ply Sweater weight (100% wool):
50g in colour 2 (beige), 20g in colour FC34 (turquoise), 20g in colour 65 (green);
Jamieson's of Shetland Spindrift (100% wool):
25g in colour 640 (blue), 20g in colour 462 (orange), 20g in colour 87 (purple) and 25g in colour 101 (black)

2mm (US 0, UK 14) double-pointed needles
3mm (US 2/3, UK 11) double-pointed needles
Stitch marker
Narrow sewing needle for knits

TENSION (GAUGE)
16 stitches and 17 rows in a 5cm (2in) square

TECHNIQUES USED
Knitting with five needles (page 82), jacquard (page 84)

PATTERN: USE CHART I (PAGE 149)

INSTRUCTIONS

Using the 2mm (US 0, UK 14) needles and blue yarn, cast on 96 sts evenly between the four needles. Place a marker on the needle to indicate the end/start of the round, and work 2 rounds in rib stitch 2 x 2 (*p2, k2*, repeat from * to * until end of round).

Next 2 rounds: using beige yarn (and leaving the blue yarn uncut), work in rib stitch 2/2.

Next 2 rounds: using blue yarn (and leaving the beige yarn uncut), work in rib stitch 2/2.

Following rounds: continue to work alternating 2 rounds of rib stitch with beige yarn and 2 rounds of rib stitch with blue yarn until there are seven complete beige stripes.

Next round: work rib stitch using blue yarn.

Next round: using 3mm (US 2/3, UK 11) needles and blue yarn, purl.

Following rounds: keeping blue as background colour, follow Chart I.

The whole pattern is worked using the same colour (beige), changing the background colour every 21 rounds, as shown in the chart. Whenever a new background colour is introduced, cut the yarn of the previous colour, leaving a length of approximately 10cm (4in), which will be woven in at the end. Once the final round of the pattern has been completed, without cutting the beige yarn, purl 2 further rounds with black yarn.

Next round: using 2mm (US 0, UK 14) needles, work rib stitch with black yarn.

Next round: using beige yarn (and leaving black yarn uncut), work in rib stitch 2/2.

Following rounds: continue to work alternating 2 rounds of rib stitch with beige yarn and 2 rounds of rib stitch with black yarn, until there are seven complete beige stripes.

Cut beige yarn, leaving approximately 10cm (4in) and work last 2 rounds using black yarn in rib stitch.

Cast off all the yarns as follows: purl those in purl, and knit those in knit.

FINISHING

Weave in the yarn ends, working them through the stitches on the reverse side.

Repeat the pattern from the beginning to complete the pair.

CHART A

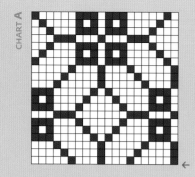

CHART B

	685
	675
	natural white
	515
	729
	567

CHART C

	101
	462
	870
	246
	1160
	243
	640
	104

CHART D

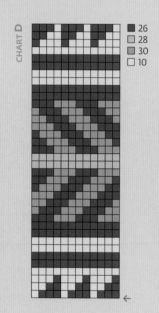

	26
	28
	30
	10

CHART E

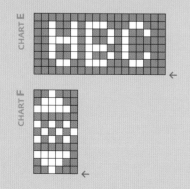

CHART F

CHART G

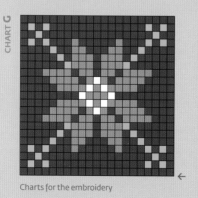

Charts for the embroidery

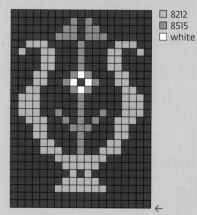

	8212
	8515
	white

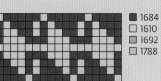

■ 1684
□ 1610
□ 1692
□ 1788

CHART I

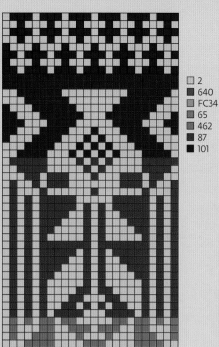

□ 2
■ 640
□ FC34
■ 65
■ 462
■ 87
■ 101

The charts should be read from right to left and from bottom to top. The arrow indicates the starting point of the piece.

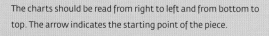

USEFUL INFORMATION

Yarns, books and links

Brands of yarn used in this book

Brooklyn Tweed (USA)
www.brooklyntweed.net

Debbie Bliss (England)
www.debbieblissonline.com

Jamieson & Smith (Scotland)
www.shetlandwoolbrokers.co.uk

Jamieson's of Shetland (Scotland)
www.jamiesonsofshetland.co.uk

Kauni (Denmark)
www.kauni.com

Katia (Spain)
www.katia.com

Limol (Portugal)
limol.pt

Mirasol (Peru)
www.mirasolperu.com

Retrosaria (Portugal)
www.retrosaria.rosapomar.com

Rosários4 (Portugal)
www.rosarios4.com

Zitron (Germany)
www.atelierzitron.de

Many of these yarns can be purchased at
Retrosaria:
Rua do Loreto, 61 - 2.o Dto
1200-090 Lisbon, Portugal
www.retrosaria.rosapomar.com

References

O Grande Livro dos Lavores (*The Great Book of Crafts*), published in the 1980s by Reader's Digest (no longer in print, but possibly available in some libraries), is still the most comprehensive knitting reference manual in Portuguese. Despite having been originally written in English, and therefore not covering Portuguese techniques, it was exceptionally well translated and remains as useful now as it was thirty years ago.

In the English language, the authors who have most inspired me are **Elizabeth Zimmermann, Cynthia Gravelle LeCount, Priscilla A. Gibson-Roberts** and **Montse Stanley**. Elizabeth Zimmermann, who was born in 1910, was renowned for the innovative way in which she wrote about and approached knitting. In one of her best-known books, *Knitting Without Tears*, she explains a logical and intuitive formula to calculate the proportions for pullovers using circular knitting, which is still widely used today. Cynthia Gravelle LeCount and Priscilla A. Gibson-Roberts are another two ground-breaking researchers in the field who helped to shine a light on traditional knitting techniques from many different parts of the world. The former researched the knitting traditions of the Andes (*Andean Folk Knitting: Traditions and techniques from Peru and Bolivia*, 1990), and the latter did extensive research into the methods used for traditional socks and pullovers (*Ethnic Socks and Stockings*, 1995 and *Knitting in the Old Way*, 2004). Finally, Montse Stanley was the author of one of the most comprehensive and interesting knitting manuals in print – the *Reader's Digest Knitter's Handbook*, and was the organizer of the historic exhibition *Mil Anys de Disseny en Punt* (*A Thousand Years of Needlepoint Design*).

Websites and blogs

Ravelry (www.ravelry.com) is the major reference site for knitters. It is a vast database constructed by users themselves, where people can look for yarns, patterns and books from all over the world. These sites are also very useful:

www.katedaviesdesigns.com
www. techknitting.blogspot.com
www. maryjanemucklestone.com
www. asplundknits.blogspot.com
www.brooklyntweed.com
www. theknittinggenie.com

Bibliography

AFONSO, João, *O Trajo nos Açores*, 2nd ed. Angra do Heroísmo, Secretaria Regional dos Assuntos Sociais, 1987.

ALMEIDA, Cláudia; BRITO, Joaquim Pais de and MELO, Patrícia, *Normas de Inventário:Tecnologia Têxtil*. Lisbon, Instituto Português dos Museus, 2007.

Artes e Tradições da Região do Porto. Lisbon, Terra Livre, 1985, p. 120.

Artes e Tradições de Évora e Portalegre. Levantamento realizado pelos Centros de Estágio de Educação Visual. Escolas Preparatórias de Évora e Portalegre. Lisbon, Terra Livre, 1980.

BASTOS, Carlos, *Indústria e Arte Têxtil*. Porto, Tipografia Portugalia, 1960.

BEL, A.; RICARD, P., *Le Travail de la Laine à Tlemcen*. Algiers, Typographie Adolphe Jourdain, 1913.

BLUTEAU, Raphael, *Vocabulario portuguez e latino, aulico, anatomico, architectonico, bellico, botanico, brasilico, comico, critico, chimico, dogmatico, dialectico, dendrologico, ecclesiastico, etymologico, economico, florifero, forense, fructifero... autorizado com exemplos dos melhores escritores portugueses, e latinos... / pelo padre D. Raphael Bluteau*. Coimbra, 1712–1728. [Online, accessed, 2012]. Available at http://www.brasiliana. usp.br/dictionary/edicao/1.

BOTELHO, João Alpuim (coord.), *Amadeu Costa: Traje e Chieira. Catálogo da Exposição do Museu do Traje de Viana do Castelo*. Viana do Castelo, Câmara Municipal de Viana do Castelo, 2011.

BUARCOS, João Brandão de, *Grandeza e Abastança de Lisboa em 1552*. Org. and notes by Joseph Felicidade Alves. Lisbon, Livros Horizonte, 1990.

BULLAR, Joseph & BULLAR, Henry, *A Winter in the Azores and a Summer at the Baths of the Furnas*. London, 2 vols., John Van Voorst - Paternoster Row, 1841–1842.

CHAVES, Luís.'...Pele e Osso... Utilidades facultadas ao homem pelos animais na sua economia', *Revista de Etnografia*. Museu de Etnografia e História. Vol. XIII, Book 1, 1969. pp. 17–104.

COMB, William, *A History of Madeira with a Series of Twenty-seven Coloured Engravings Illustrative of the Costumes, Manners, and Occupations of the Inhabitants of that Island*. London: B. Ackermann, 1821.

Como Trajava o Povo Português. Exposição integrada no Festinatel/91 – 5.o Festival Internacional de Folclore. Org. Rita Maria Bouça, s.l., Ed. INATEL, 1991.

CORREIA, Mário, *Pauliteiros de Miranda (Cércio). Viagem a Londres*. Royal Albert Hall, Janeiro, 1934. Sendim, Centro de Música Tradicional Sons da Terra, 2008.

CORREIA, Vergílio, *Etnografia Artística Portuguesa*. Barcelos, Companhia Editora do Minho, 1937.

CORREIA, Vergílio, 'A indústria popular de Mondim"das meias"'. *Terra Portuguesa*. 2.o vol., ano 1, n.o 7, August 1916, pp. 50–52.

COSTA, Maria da Glória Azevedo Martins da, *O Traje Poveiro*. Sep. do *Boletim Cultural Póvoa de Varzim*, Vol. XIX, no. 2, 1980 Póvoa de Varzim, 1980.

COSTA, Mário Alberto Nunes, *Algumas notas sobre a Indústria de Lanifícios no Alentejo*. Lisbon, 1992.

COVARRUBIAS HOROZCO, Sebastián de, *Tesoro de la Lengua Castellana, O Española*. Madrid, 1611. [Online, accessed 2012]. Available at http://fondosdigitales.us.es/fondos/ libros/765/16/tesoro-de-la-lengua-castellana-o-espanola/.

CRESPO, Hugo Miguel, 'Trajar as Aparências, Vestir para Ser: o Testemunho da Pragmática de 1609', in SOUSA, Gonçalo Vasconcelos and (coord.), *O Luxo na Região do Porto ao Tempo de Filipe II de Portugal (1610)*, Porto, Universidade Católica Editora, 2012, pp. 93–148.

CUNHA, Armando Santinho & FERREIRA, Fernando Eduardo Rodrigues, *Vida e Morte na Época de D. Afonso Henriques*. Lisbon, Hugin, 1998.

DAVIES, Kate, 'Fishing, Knitting, and the Invention of Tradition' [Online, accessed January 2013]. Available at http://barantuil.tumblr.com/arangansey.

DIAS, Luís Fernando de Carvalho, *Os lanifícios na política económica do conde da Ericeira*. Lisbon, 1953.

DILLMONT, Thérèse de, *Encyclopédie des Ouvrages de Dames*. Mulhouse, Éditions Th. de Dillmont, 1951 [1886].

FELICIANO, María Judith, 'Muslim shrouds for Christian kings? A reassessment of Andalusi textiles in thirteenth-century Castillian life and ritual' in *Under the Influence: Questioning the Comparative in Medieval Castile*. eds. Cynthia Robinson & Leyla Rouhi. Leiden, 2005, pp. 101–132.

FERREIRA, Ana Maria Pereira, *Importação e Comércio Têxtil em Portugal no século XV, 1385 a 1481*. Lisbon, INCM, 1983.

FERREIRA, Fernando Eduardo Rodrigues, 'Escavações do ossário de S. Vicente de Fora. Seu relacionamento com a história de Lisboa', *Lisbon. Revista Municipal*, Edição da C. M. L., ano 44, 2nd series, no.4, 2nd quarter of 1983, pp. 5–36.

FONSECA, Lília da, *O Tricot sem Mestre*. Vol. 1, Lisbon, Livraria Bertrand, 1957.

FREITAS, Maria Constança Múria de,"Palavras e expressões sobre Vestuário no Cancioneiro Geral de Garcia de Resende'. *Boletim de Filologia*, VIII, Lisbon, 1947, pp. 67–120, IX, Lisbon, 1948, pp. 12–149.

GARCIA, João Carlos, 'Os Têxteis no Portugal dos Séculos XV e XVI'. Finisterra. *Revista Portuguesa de Geografia*, 21.42, 1986, pp. 327–344.

GARCIA-BERMEJO, Ángela López; MAGANTO HURTADO, Esther; MERINO ARROYO, Carlos, *La Indumentaria Tradicional Segoviana*. Segovia, Caja Segovia, 2000.

GARRETT, João Baptista da Silva Leitão de Almeida, Da Educação. *Cartas dirigidas a uma senhora illustre encarregada da instituição de uma joven princeza*. 2nd ed., Porto, Viúva Moré, 1867.

GERALDES, Alice, *Castro Laboreiro e Soajo. Habitação, Vestuário e Trabalho da Mulher*. Lisbon, National Service for Parks, Reserves and Heritage Landscape, 1979.

GIBSON-ROBERTS, Priscilla A, *Ethnic Socks and Stockings: A Compendium of Eastern Design and Technique*. Sioux Falls, Elaine Rowley, 1995.

GONÇALVES, Luísa; GOMES, Duarte, 'António Martins, de Santana. Quando é um homem a fazer barretes' in *Traços da Tradição Madeirense*. Funchal, Ed. O Liberal, 2012, pp. 103–109.

GONÇALVES, Luísa; GOMES, Duarte, *O Barrete de Orelhas. Breves Apontamentos*. Ed. Junta de Freguesia da Camacha, 2011.

GONZÁLEZ MENA, María Angeles (org.), *Colección Pedagógico Textil de la Universidad Complutense de Madrid*. Madrid, Consejo Superior de la Universidad Complutense de Madrid, 1994.

GRAÇA, António dos Santos, *O Poveiro*. 1932.

GUERREIRO, Manuel Viegas, *Projecto Tecnologia e Tradição: informatização de Arquivos Etnográficos*. Centro de Tradições Populares Portuguesas. [Online, accessed 2011]. Available at http://ww3.fl.ul.pt/unidades/centros/ctp/tecnotrad/index.htm.

HENRIQUES, M. Borges de F., *A Trip to the Azores or Western Islands*. Boston, Lee and Shepard, 1867.

KIM, Tai Whan, *The Portuguese Element in Japanese: A Critical Survey with Glossary*. Coimbra, Faculdade de Letras da Universidade de Coimbra, Instituto de Estudos Românicos, 1976.

LAMAS, Maria, *As Mulheres do Meu País*. 2nd ed, Lisbon, Caminho, 2003 [1948–50].

LECOUNT, Cynthia Gravelle, *Andean Folk Knitting: Traditions and Techniques from Peru and Bolivia*. Saint Paul, Dos Tejedoras Fiber Arts Publications, 1990.

LIMA, Fernando Castro Pires de (dir.), *A Arte Popular em Portugal*. Lisbon, Verbo, 1959–1963.

LIMA, Fernando Castro Pires de (dir.), *A Arte Popular em Portugal. Ilhas Adjacentes e Ultramar*, Vol. I. Lisbon, Verbo, 1968–1975.

LIMA, Marcelino, 'Indústrias caseiras' in Álbum Açoriano, Lisbon, 1903, pp. 455–458.

Livro dos Regimetos dos Officiaes mecanicos da mui nobre e sepre leal cidade de Lixboa (1572). Pub. e pref. Vergílio Correia. Coimbra, Imprensa da Univ. Coimbra, 1926.

MACEDO, José Borges de, *Problemas de História da Indústria Portuguesa no século XVIII*. 2nd ed. Lisbon, Quercu, 1982.

MADAHIL, António Gomes da Rocha, *Trajos e Costumes Populares Portugueses do Século XIX, em litografias de Joubert, Macphail e Palhares*. Porto, ed. Panorama, 1968.

MADUREIRA, Nuno Luís (ed.), *História do Trabalho e das Ocupações*. Vol. 1, A Indústria Têxtil. Lisbon, Editorial Celta, 2001.

MARREIROS, Glória, *Viveres, saberes e fazeres tradicionais da mulher algarvia*. Lagos, 1995.

MARTINS, Francisco (ed.), *Guimarães. O Labor da Grei. Publicação comemorativa da Exposição Industrial e Agrícola Concelhia realizada em Agosto de 1923*. Guimarães, 1928.

MAY, Florence Lewis, *Hispanic Lace and Lacemaking*. New York, The Hispanic Society of America, 1939.

MELLO, José Maria de Campos, *Lans e Lanifícios*. Coimbra, França Amado Editor, 1907.

Mil Anys de Disseny en Punt, org. Centre de Documentació i Museu Tèxtil. Terrassa, 1997.

NEVES, José Acúrsio das, *Noções Históricas, Económicas e administrativas sobre a produção, e manufactura das sedas em Portugal, e particularmente sobre a Real Fábrica do suburbio do Rato, e suas annexas*. Lisbon, Impressão Régia, 1827.

O Grande Livro dos Lavores. Lisbon, selections of Reader's Digest, 1985.

O Traje do Litoral Português, org. Ethnographic Museum and Archeological Dr. Joaquim Manso. Nazaré, Nazaré Town Council, 2003.

OLIVEIRA, Cristóvão Rodrigues de, *Lisboa em 1551. Sumário em que brevemente se contêm algumas coisas assim eclesiásticas como seculares que há na cidade de Lisboa (1551)*. Presentation and notes by José Felicidade Alves. Lisbon, Livros Horizonte, 1987.

OLIVEIRA, Fernando Baptista, Método de Fazer Malhas. O 'Tricot' em todas as modalidades. A técnica. Os pontos. O vestuário. Os moldes. Lisbon Editorial 'O Século', 1952.

OLIVEIRA, Fernando José Cunha de, O Vestuário Português ao Tempo da Expansão. Séculos XV e XVI. Ed. Grupo de Trabalho do Min. Educação for the commemorations of the Portuguese discoveries. 1993.

OLIVEIRA, Fernanda Teigas de, Tricotar à Mão e à Máquina. Lisbon, Edições Fada do Lar, date unknown.

PALLA, Maria José, Do Essencial e do Supérfluo. Estudo lexical do traje e adornos em Gil Vicente. Lisbon, Estampa, 1992.

PARKS, Clara, The Knitter's Book of Yarn: The Ultimate Guide to Choosing, Using, and Enjoying Yarn. New York, Potter Craft, 2007.

PEREIRA, Benjamim Enes, Bibliografia Analítica de Etnografia Portuguesa. Lisbon, Instituto de Alta Cultura, 1965.

PEREIRA, Benjamim Enes, 'O canhão de fazer meia'. Trabalhos de Antropologia e Etnologia. Porto. Vol. XVIII, Fasc. 1-2, 1960–1961.

PEREIRA, João Manuel Esteves (1872–1944), Subsídios para a História da Indústria Portuguesa. Com um ensaio económicosocial sobre as corporações e mesteres por Carlos da Fonseca. Lisbon Guimarães Editores, 1979.

PESSANHA, Sebastião, 'Bonecos de Estremoz', A Terra Portuguesa, 1, Lisbon, 1916, pp. 105–109.

PIMENTEL, Alberto, A Extremadura Portugueza. Vol. I, O Ribatejo. Lisbon, Empreza da Historia de Portugal, 1908.

PINTO, António Joaquim de Gouveia, Exame Crítico e Histórico sobre os direitos estabelecidos pela legislação antiga, e moderna, tanto pátria, como subsidiária, e das nações vizinhas, e cultas, relativamente aos expostos, ou engeitados, para servir de base a um Regulamento geral administrativo, a favor dos mesmos (...). Lisbon, Tipografia da Acedemia Real das Sciencias, 1828.

PIRES, Ana, 'As Rendas e Bordados da Beira de Maria Júlia Antunes' in Mãos. Revista de Artes e Ofícios, 33.

PIRES, Ana, 'Produções têxteis artesanais portuguesas' in Fios. Formas e memórias dos tecidos, rendas e bordados. Lisbon, IEFP, 2009, pp. 9–25.

PIRES, Ana; Gonçalves, Eduardo; GASPAR, Fernando (coord.), Artesanato da Região Centro. Traditional and Contemporary Crafts in Central Portugal. Coimbra, Institute of Employment and Professional Training, 1992.

RIBEIRO, Luís da Silva, 'O trajo popular terceirense' in Obras. Vol. I, Etnografia Açoriana. Angra do Heroísmo, Instituto Histórico da Ilha Terceira, 1982, pp. 205–214.

Projecto Tecnologia e Tradição: Informatização de Arquivos Etnográficos. Centro de Tradições Populares Portuguesas, Manuel Viegas Guerreiro. [Online, accessed 2012]. Available at http://ww3.fl.ul.pt/unidades/centros/ctp/tecnotrad/index.htm

RIBEIRO, Margarida, 'Breve comentário sobre rocas e técnicas de fiar e retorcer' in Boletim Cultural da Assembleia Distrital de Lisboa, 91, Vol. 2, 1989, pp. 149–162.

ROXO, Maria José, Rendas 'por música' de duas agulhas feitas à mão. Porto, Civilização, 1986.

RUTT, Richard, A History of Hand Knitting. London, Batsford, 1987.

SEQUEIRA, Joana, MELO, Arnaldo Sousa, 'A mulher na produção têxtil portuguesa tardo-medieval'. Medievalista, 11 (January – June 2012). [Online, accessed 24.10.2012]. Available at http://www2.fcsh.unl.pt/iem/medievalista/MEDIEVALISTA11\ textil1105.html.

SILVA, Antonio Moraes, Diccionario da lingua portugueza – recompilado dos vocabularios impressos ate agora, e nesta segunda edição novamente emendado e muito acrescentado, por ANTONIO DE MORAES SILVA. Lisbon, Typographia Lacerdina, 1813. [Online, accessed in 2012]. Available at http://www.brasiliana.usp.br/Bbd/handle/1918/00299210.

SILVEIRA, Pedro da, José Leite de Vasconcellos nas Ilhas de Baixo. Seara Nova, 1959.

SOALHEIRO, João; MONTEIRO, Paula & SERRANO, Carmo, Tecidos Medievais. Lisbon, Instituto Português de Conservação e Restauro, 2004.

SOARES, Maria Micaela Ramos Trindade, As meias dos maiorais da borda d'água. Reprint of the Actas do Colóquio sobre artesanato (Coimbra, 8–11 November 1879). Coimbra, Serviços Municipais de Cultura e Turismo & IPPC, 1982.

SOUSA, Alberto, O Trajo Popular em Portugal, nos séculos XVI a XIX. Lisbon, 1924.

SOUSA, António Teixeira de; CAMPOS, Maria Teresa Themudo (coord.), Artesanato da Região Norte: Traditional and Contemporary Crafts in Northern Portugal. 2nd ed., Porto, Instituto do Emprego e Formação Profissional, 1991.

STANLEY, Montse, Reader's Digest Knitter's Handbook: A Comprehensive Guide to the Principles and Techniques of Hand Knitting. 7th ed. Singapore, Reader's Digest, 2010.

STANLEY, Montse, 'Mil anys de punt. Puralisme i interrogants' in Mil Anys de Disseny en Punt, org. Centre de Documentació i Museu Tèxtil. Terrassa, 1997, pp. 35–66.

TEIXEIRA, Madalena Braz (coord.), Traje do Algarve. Orla Marítima. Museu Nacional do Traje, IPM, 2001.

TEIXEIRA, Magdalene Braz (Commissioner), *Trajes Míticos da Cultura Regional Portuguesa, Museu Nacional do Traje*. Lisbon. Lisbon European Capital of Culture '94, 1994.

THOMAS, Mary, *Mary Thomas's Knitting Book*. New York, S. D. [1938].

THOMPSON, Gladys, *Patterns for Guernseys, Jerseys & Arans: Fishermen Sweaters from the British Isles*. 3rd ed. New York, Dover Publications, 1979.

TOCHA, Gonçalo (production), *É na Terra não É na Lua*. 2011. Film.

Tratado de Trabalhos de Agulha. Rio de Janeiro. H. Lombaerts & C., Editores, 1890.

TURNAU, Irena, *History of Knitting Before Mass Production*. Warsaw, PAN IHKM, 1991.

VASCONCELOS, José Leite de, 'Apetrechos de meia' in *Opúsculos*. Vol. V, Etnografia I. Lisbon, Imprensa Nacional de Lisboa, 1938, pp. 442–454.

VASCONCELOS, José Leite de, 'Etnografia Estremenha', *Boletim de Etnografia*, II, 2, Lisbon, Imprensa Nacional de Lisboa, 1920, pp.44–51.

VASCONCELOS, José Leite de, 'Estampas Etnográficas', *Boletim de Etnografia*, I, Lisbon, Imprensa Nacional de Lisboa, 1920, pp.53–58.

VASCONCELOS, José Leite de, *Etnografia Portuguesa. Tentame de sistematização*. Vol. VI, Lisbon, INCM, 1975.

VASCONCELOS, José Leite de, 'Leiteiro e carapuças da Madeira', *Boletim de Etnografia*, I, Lisbon, 1920, pp.13–14.

VASCONCELOS, José Leite de, *Memórias de Mondim da Beira. Para a História do Concelho deste Nome*. 2nd ed. facsimile of the 1933 edition, Lisbon, Imprensa Nacional, 2002.

VASCONCELOS, Maria Emília Sena de, *A Importância das meias no traje, no lirismo, na vida popular do Alto Minho*. Viana do Castelo, 1996.

VITERBO, Joaquim de Santa Rosa de, *Elucidário das palavras, termos e frases que em Portugal antigamente se usaram e que hoje regularmente se ignoram: obra indispensável para entender sem erro os documentos mais raros e preciosos que entre nós se conservam / Publicado em Benefício da Litheratura Portugueza Por Fr. Joaquim de Santa Rosa Viterbo. ... – 2nd ed. journal, correcta e copiosamente addicionada de novos vocábulos, observações e notas críticas com um índice remissivo*. Lisbon, A. J. Fernandes Lopes, 1865.

WRIGHT, Mary, *Cornish Guernseys & Knit-frocks*. Herefordshire, 1979.

Credits

Every effort has been made to credit copyright holders. We apologize for any involuntary omissions, and are happy to correct them in future editions of this book.

The history of knitting

1 Patrimonio Nacional España; **2** Layout: Maria José Taxinha & Isabel Uva. Photography: Jorge Oliveira. Sé Patriarcal de Lisboa. General Directorate of Cultural Heritage, Division of Documentation, Communication and Computing – Library for Conservation and Museums; **3** Tesouro-Museu da Sé de Braga; **4** Layout: Maria José Taxinha & Isabel Uva. Photography: Palma. Sao Vicente de Fora convent. General Directorate of Cultural Heritage, Division of Documentation, Communication and Computing – Library for Conservation and Museums; **5** Layout: Maria José Taxinha & Isabel Uva. Photography: Palma. Sao Vicente de Fora convent. General Directorate of Cultural Heritage, Division of Documentation, Communication and Computing – Library of Conservation and Museums; **6** 'Der Besuch der Engel' – doppelflügeliges Altarretabel der Petrikirche in Buxtehude - Innenseite des rechten Altarflügels. bpk. Hamburger Kunsthalle. Elke Walford bpk; **7** María con el niño rodeada por Santas y Ángeles. Nicolás y Martín de Zahórtiga. 1460. Museo de la Colegiata de Santa Maria de Borja; **8** Academia de Ciências de Lisboa – Lisbon; **9** Museu Nacional de Arte Antiga. Photography: Luisa Oliveira. General Directorate of Cultural Heritage/Archive of photographic documentation; **10, 11, 12** Private collection of Rosa Pomar.

Portuguese knitting

1 Joana Maria Osório; **2** Matthew Fung. Photographer from Canada. http://matthewfungphotography.com; **3, 13, 16, 17, 25, 50** Rosa Pomar; **4** private collection of Rita Forjaz. Rosa Pomar; **5** Knitting hooks. Museu Nacional de Arqueologia. Photography: José Pessoa. General directorate of Cultural heritage/Archive of photographic documentation; **6** Design by Fernando Galhano. Museu Nacional de Etnologia. General Directorate of Cultural Heritage/Archive of photographic documentation; **7** Private collection of Cláudia Mestre. Rosa Pomar; **8** Museu de Arte Popular. Photography: Luisa Oliveira. General Directorate of Cultural Heritage/Archive of photographic documentation; **9** Private collections of Rosa Pomar and Ana Châteauneuf Faria; **10** Private collection of Claudia Mestre. Rosa Pomar; **11** IRPA-KIK, Brussels; **12** Woman in festival attire leans on stone W. Robert Moore/ National Geographic Society/Corbis; **14** © Jorge Barros; **15** Amadeu Ferrari. Photographic Archives of Lisbon city council; **18** National Museum of Ethnology. Photography: António Rento. General Directorate of Cultural Heritage/Archive of photographic documentation; **19** National Museum of Ethnology. Photography: António Rento. General Directorate of Cultural Heritage/Archive of photographic documentation; **20** National Museum of Ethnology. Photography: António Rento. General Directorate of Cultural Heritage/Archive of photographic documentation; **21** Artes e Tradições da Região do Porto. Lisbon, Terra Livre, 1985. Author unknown; **22** Helena Corrêa de Barros. Photographic Archives of Lisbon city council; **23** Como Trajava o Povo Português. Exhibition held at Festinatel/91. Org. Rita Maria Bouça, s.l., Ed. INATEL, 1991. Author unknown; **24** Private collection. Rosa Pomar; **26** National Museum of Ethnology. Photography: António Rento. General Directorate of Cultural Heritage/Archive of photographic documentation; **27** Bedford Whaling Museum; **28** National Museum of Ethnology. Photography: Luisa Oliveira. General Directorate of Cultural Heritage/Archive of photographic documentation; **29** Biblioteca Nacional. E.A. 67 V; **30** Arminius T. Haeberle/National Geographic Society/Corbis; **31** Arquivo do Centro de Tradições Populares Portuguesas da Faculdade de Letras da Universidade e Lisboa; **32** Bedford Whaling Museum; **33** Sr. José Ferreira. Photography: Tiago Pereira; **34** Private collection of Rosa Pomar; **35** Biblioteca Nacional. D.S. XIX–274; **36** Biblioteca Nacional. H.G. 18803 V; **37** Private collection of Catarina Portas; **38** Museu Municipal de Etnografia e História da Póvoa de Varzim; **39** Cinemateca Portuguesa – Museu do Cinema; **40** Museu de Arte Popular. Photography: Paulo Cintra/Laura Castro Caldas. General Directorate of Cultural Heritage/ Archive of photographic documentation; Photography; **41** Seventeen Magazine. August 1962. Private Collection of Rosa Pomar; **42** National Museum of Archeology. Photography: Luísa Oliveira. General Directorate of Cultural Heritage/ Archive of photographic documentation; **43** National Museum of Ethnology. Photography: Luísa Oliveira. General Directorate of Cultural Heritage/Archive of photographic documentation; **44** Private collection of Rosa Pomar; **45** National Museum of Ethnology. Photography: Luisa Oliveira. General Directorate of Cultural Heritage/Archive of photographic documentation; **46** Patrimonio Nacional España; **47** Private Collection. Rosa Pomar; **48** Private Collection of Ana Vaz. Rosa Pomar; **49** Exhibition of the Portuguese World (1940), Lisbon, Portugal. Mário Novais. Fundação Calouste Gulbenkian – Biblioteca de Arte.

Experts

1 Sra. Avelina. Photography Tiago Pereira; **2** Sra Isabel Ferreira. Photography Tiago Pereira; **3** Sra Paula de Jesus Monteiro. Photography Tiago Pereira.

Models

pp. 99, 101, 102, 103, 104, 105, 106, 110, 111, 112, 113, 115, 116, 117, 118, 119, 120, 121, 122, 123, 126, 127, 129, 130, 134, 135, 138, 144, 145, 146, 147 Rosa Pomar; pp. 107, 108, 109, 128, 131, 133, 140, 141, 144, 145 Diane Gazeau; pp. 114, 142, 143 Tiago Pereira.

Cover, back cover, pp. 10, 11, 26, 27, 64, 65, 70, 72, 74, 84, 85, 96, 97, 150, 151 Rosa Pomar.

Acknowledgments

This book would not have seen the light of day without the help of my parents, Alexandre Pomar and Luísa Cortesão, without the help of Tiago Pereira and Filipe Pacheco, and without the joy of my daughters Elvira and Amélia.

I would like to thank Simona Cattabiani for believing in me, for inviting me to undertake this project, and for never giving up. Thanks also to Nuno Cravo for his attention to detail and constant support in the final straight, when it seemed that almost everything had been done yet there was still so much to do.

The author's personal and professional acknowledgments:
Adélia Garcia (Caçarelhos)
Ana Pires
Ana Vaz
Beatriz Silva
Bela Celeste (Alcáçovas)
Carolina Magalhães da Costa (Mezio)
Clara Vaz Pinto (Museu Nacional do Traje)
Cláudia Mestre
Daniela Araújo
Deolinda Carneiro (Museu Municipal de Etnografia e História da Póvoa de Varzim)
Deolinda Ferreira da Costa (Mezio)
Diane Gazeau
Elsa Ferraz (Museu Nacional do Traje)
Genoveva Grave (Aldeia da Serra)
Hernâni Matos
Isabel Ferreira (Ribeiro Frio)
Isabel Sá (Associação Aldeia)
Isolda Rosário (Rosários4)
Joana Caetano
Joana Osório
Luísa Valério (Alvito)
Maria Adelaide Sousa Oliveira
Maria de Fátima Sampaio Furtado (Ponta Delgada)
Maria de Lurdes Magalhães Quintans (Associação Etnográfica e Social do Montemuro)
Maria Felismina Pereira (Aldeia da Serra)
Maria João Velhinho (Redondo)
Maria do Rosário Figueiredo (Santarém)
Marina Tavares Dias
Militina Tereso (Aldeia da Serra)
Nuno Borges de Araújo
Paula de Jesus Monteiro (Duas Igrejas)
Paula Monteiro (Instituto dos Museus e da Conservação)
Pedro Augusto (Museu Nacional de Etnologia)
Rita Forjaz
Rosário Caeiro
Rui Camacho
Sandra Coelho
Suzana Ruano
Teresa de Jesus Martins (Aldeia da Serra)
Teresa Senra Simões (Bucos)

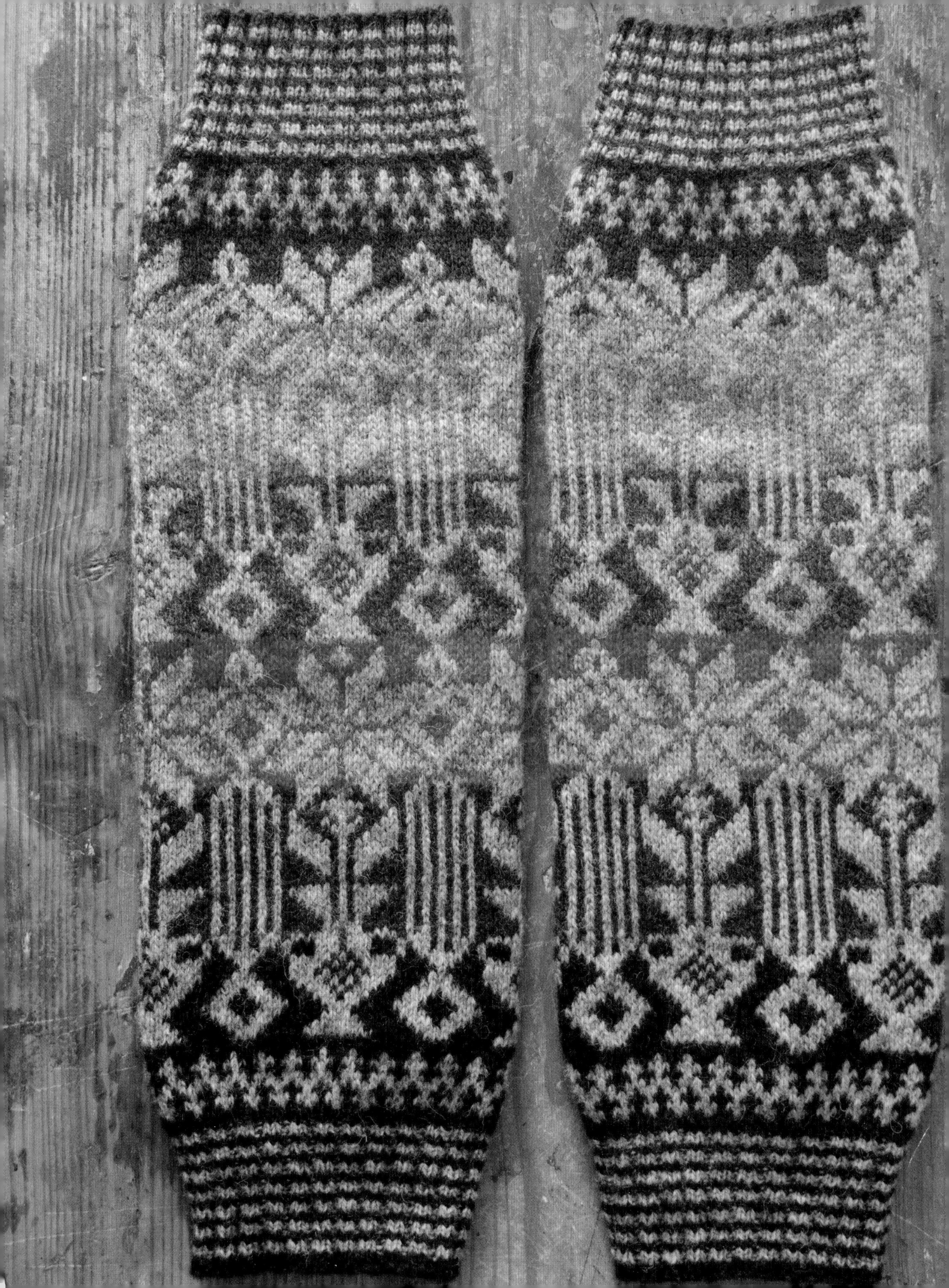